CAMBETH

JAMES W MONTGOMERY

Year of Completion 2008:
James William Montgomery Register of Copyrights, United States of America
ISNB: 978-0-578-63090-8
Registration Number
TXu 1-691-554
Effective Date of Registration: February 24, 2009
Philadelphia, Pennsylvania

Skipfamu@aol.com

For so long I have loved, struggled, and prayed with God about this game universally known as baseball. As a toddler my mother was enormously proud of me catching a ball ricocheting from high on the dining room wall. It was my uncle Genie who talked about the game with much humor, passion and words that would inspire. That, along with my strong will to break out of the families impoverished surroundings helped to fuel my desire. I will never forget how he was so supremely delighted with Spahn, Aaron, Matthews, and Bruton the old Milwaukee Braves. Following along with my uncle to Philadelphia's Connie Mack Stadium to see them, I instantly became a slave unto baseball because baseball is not beholden unto time.

To the Reader

Cambeth is composed in the genre of Philadelphia neighborhood aka "Yo Philly" street language. The script is enjoined with the literary flavor and quaint structure of early modern English language. The Cambeth writing style, includes idioms slang and cultural expressions from the 1960's up to and including the 21ˢᵗ century i.e., the third millennium. These writings are combined with the American aughts* in conjunction with the British noughts* of the 1600's. The script is intertwined with so-called Shakespeare colloquialism and the artistic explosion and appreciation in poetry, literature, and theatre of the Elizabethan era. My approach and interpretation to Macbeth via Cambeth, gives it a literary uniqueness that I believe suites a delicious flavor of spelling baseball into classic Shakespeare.

*American aughts: a reference to the first decade of a century in American English, such as 2000's

*British noughties: January 1, 2000, BBC listed noughties…moniker for the new decade of the century.

Shakespeare Re-Mixed

WHY THIS?...WHY NOT!

The Purpose of this remix is to show that William Shakespeare still rules. For centuries he has armed us most eloquently with awesome linguistic tools. At the time of his presence his scripts were frothy and fluent. He was enjoyed by all classes of people, even school capacities of few truants.

Yet, in the twenty first century human writings took on a profoundly new look. People spouted new axioms called "twitter" and "text", or for many the popular "face-book". This expanded the world's communications vaster than the three fifth's that is wet. You know where the next line is going, all because of the extraordinary inter-net.

The tide was now rolling, you could say that the "word" surf was up. Swirling around with this here tempest was old William in a proper English teacup. However, his classroom popularity today is waning, because somehow classical reading is in a drought. While in certain distressed districts he's not even getting a partial shout out!

In his general he's still chief, though a little tweaking will adjust the matter. Shakespeare likely would have done what it takes, to keep his works relevant and devoid of the scatter. By "hang ten" the new wave showing that he gets this false fake. While cooking his classic recipes that offer the old shake with a spicy new bake.

Now he's making his return, like all reincarnated great stage players do. Coming in fully remixed, and with dramatics to cover the world's beautiful hew. So, roll with it, or get rolled on are your only choices you see. Presented by "the linguistic thief' whose want is to bring William Shakespeare a new glee.

James William Montgomery

AKA "Bakespeare

CAMBETH

Cast:

Ernie, Owner of the Mustangs
Monty/Skip, (North Philly #1 centerfielder)
Tony, player/player (both son's of Ernie)

Willie, (South Philly #1 centerfielder)
Hartie, seasoned Mustang veteran

Dawson, (Hall of Fame Major Leaguer)
Clyde, (player/manager) Mustangs
JoJo, (minor leaguer)
Durant (college player/coach)
FAMU Larry, Mustang Capt.
Luke, (ex-pro/college coach)
FAMU

Goldie, Willie's wife Lady "D,"

Dawson's wife
Tenderhearted Lady, (helper to Goldie)
Heatherkat, queen of magic Three Shorties
Stormin' Norman, son of Hartie

Little Hall All-Star, South Jersey
Young Hall, his daughter

Lofton, (player) valet to Willie Boy, son of Dawson
Dr.Johnson, Physician Warlord, 2nd command (gang) Sal, (Dawson's son's name)
A Bellhop

Jake, (an old man) Premonitions

Lord Bethea, (league's best pitcher)-Players, All-Stars, Killers, Attendants,

Bearer, Setting: Philadelphia and Tallahassee, (USA) the Twentieth century.

Written by James W. Montgomery aka, (Skip)
Completed 08.31. MMVIII 12:27p

CAMBETH PROLOGUE

Roget's Thesaurus describes war as, competition and conflict. The conflicts of competition can be played out on the battlefields of war, or the grassy fields of baseball. One is the killing field of death, the other is the diamond field of dreams. The clutches of competition for both are uniquely mirrored with their conflicts. Cambeth is the story of the rise and fall of warring baseball.

C-ompromise, there can be none,
O-nly the strong survives down to one.
M-en and women are all equal to compete,
P-rizes to the winner, to the loser a delete.
E-nter the arena seeking fortune and fame,
T-aking the victory that allures the eyes without shame.
I-nvested is the loss with only a tantalizing pawn,
T-ally on through the battle, maybe from dusk till dawn.
I-dolizing every action to allow memory a life through midnight's blue,
O-h, the contest proved you adeptly worthy, and oh so decidedly true.
N-abbing the golden ring of party, and the blessing of the feast,
!- with the merriment and mirth, till the fire rises in the East.

and

C-ounter punching is the mandate, in every situation it's the must,
O-r the battle be lost quickly, and the triumph be a bust.
N-ever hedging to the opponent; attack vociferously and strong,
F-orced submission is their judgment, happy trails is their song.
L-ack luster is no winning, spoils are as sweet as honey dew,
I-mplausable not to the mind, that knows well it to be true.
C-ontagion is the outcome, that seeks another door,
T-o taunt and tame till tempered, thus are the winds of war.

TABLE OF CONTENTS

ACT ONE: PLAY BALL

SCENE 1

[Walking through the park under dark gray skies. Enter Three Shorties.]

First Shortie.   When are you all gonna come back to the ball field?

When it's snowing, the wind blowing or after your meal?

Second Shortie. When your momma lets you go out?

That's probably after you clean the house, no doubt.

Third Shortie. Hopefully, before the hot noon sun,

that will bake us crisp and done.

First Shortie.   Where the spot.

Second Shortie. A place of no bereft.

Third Shortie. That would be Cambeth.

First Shortie.   I'll be there my kitty.

All. Frog beckons -(shouting) Solid! *   Right is wrong, and wrong is right.

Flutter through the grease and dirty night.

SCENE 2

[A gas station near Tioga. * French horns sounding. Enter Ernie, Skip/Monty, Tony, Clyde, with players, greeting a smashed* Warlord.*

Ernie. Who is that? The deal is, by the way you look, they must be rumbling with
the Tioga T's.

Skip.   This is the warlord. Who like a true main man was rockin'.* He took my
slack* and saved my back. Yo, you the bomb. You my son, if you don't ever get
none. Give the kid the sweet deets of the bang, - just before you left

Warlord. Both sides was kickin' it, like two heavyweights locked in a clench two
together, showing their skills. Them boys from the Valley,* who you know are
our arches* by nature. They swooped from around the corner. Some had bats
and pipes. I also thought I saw some shanks and pistols. Man, they showed up
like a crack head* at a rock concert. Still their stuff was weak. For "Kick butt

"Sonny"- he's got the right name, stepped right to "Troubles"... put his hands up, and shoe shined him till he knocked him out! It was like waxing an "old

solid: all's well. Tioga: neighborhood. smashed: beat up. warlord: 2nd in command. rockin': fighting. slack: taking the weight. Valley: gang in north Philadelphia. arches: arch enemies. crack head: one who uses crack cocaine.

	man comfort"* with a smile from head to heel.
Ernie.	Damn brother, that boy was representing.
Warlord.	It looked like we were seeing a little daylight. Then things began to tighten up and get a little uncomfortable. Listen "Bub" listen. Just as soon as it looked like we were going to run them boys back up to the Valley, their lord, checking things out, hollered something and these new dudes showed up from nowhere and started rockin'* with them, on their side.
Ernie.	Did get with this our two Runners* Willie and Hartie?
Warlord.	Absolutely! As midgets giants, or seals the shark. Truthfully though, but I gotta tell you, they were like two sprinters in second gear. Man, they double clutched on them boys. Expect they meant to hurt'um. I ain't seen nothing like it since Vietnam. I can't say-however, I'm about to fall out, my lumps need some ice.
Ernie.	Listening to you, I can see that you were knuckling by your battle scars. Get him to medics. Who's that coming?

[Exit Warlord, helped.]

[Enter JoJo.]

Skip/Monty.	What's up old head?
Clyde.	Look how wide his eyes are. He looks like he's going to tell you something weird.

JoJo.	Heaven spare His Majesty!
Ernie.	Where are you coming from, old head?
JoJo.	From Westmoreland, your Greatness, where the Valley done got thick as molasses, and everybody ran in the house. Girard himself with mad numbers... helped by that most treacherous traitor "young boy Hank," began to kick butt till the "Knuckle King"* with his process* wrapped ... stepped to him like a man, toe to toe, blow for blow - wingin' that sucker, and to finish we won the fight!

*old man comfort: a popular dress shoe, that was distinctive by its white stitched sole. rockin' (slang) - fighting. runner: the top-ranking leader of a gang. Knuckle King: a reference to Willie. process: chemically treated hair, so as to relax it into a straightened condition.

Ernie.	That's Boss, that's Boss!
JoJo.	So now, Seibert, Girard's sovereign, wants to sham.* However, we didn't let him off the hook until we chased them down the avenue, and they gave us ten gallons of wine.
Ernie.	We do not have to worry about "Young boy Hank" coming around here again, messing around. Hurry, go tell everyone that he is done, and his former interests now belong to Willie.
JoJo.	I'll take care of it.
Ernie.	Hank has been tanked, Hot Willie is now cool and chilly.

SCENE 3

[A vacant lot. Fireworks blasting. Enter Three Shorties.]

First Shortie.	Where have y'all scallywags* been?

Second Shortie. Swattin' flies.

Third Shortie. Yo sister, what about you?

First Shortie. A truck driver's grandmother had a bag of wet peanuts in her hand, justa chewing and chewing. "Hunks up,"* I said." Haul "a" Shortie, you sawed off little so in so." She replies. Her son's gone down 95* trying to master the road, but in a flatbed. I'll watch it roll and like a snake with a swale, okay, okay and okay.

Second Shortie. Talk on.

First Shortie. You're too fair.

Third Shortie. Yeah, rap on.

First Shortie. Here's the rest, as with the movement of time,
all the rest will fall in line,
I control the light house beam to shape and game his dream.
Robbing the thinks within the head,
the man no mind is all but dead. Dragging each day, seven twenty-four,

*sham: taking low. scallywag: weird girl. hunks up: wanting some. 95: interstate hwy.

till he thinks and shouts, no more no more! Though his statue be the manly form,

all around will cast a thunderous storm-- can you dig it!

Second Shortie.   What you got, what you got?

First Shortie. Here I have a brake cable,
crashed like a party, he'll drive off the table.

Third Shortie. The beat, the beat!
Willie comes down the street.

Todas.   The sawed off Shortie's step by step sail the sea of tears they wept,
put it all into effect.

I'll span two, and you do to, and twice again, to make up six. Silence! The plan's affixed.

[Enter Willie and Hartie]

Willie. What an oxymoron day I have never seen before.

Hartie. How far is it to the playground? Yo, what's this, these half pints, and dressed like a peacock, they don't look like normal people on this earth, but they're on it. You all alright, or should this man ask? I think you understand me, all have a crooked finger in her big ear. You're shaped like women, and yet, your bald heads won't allow me to call you that which you are.

Willie. Shout out if you are able. What the hell are you?

First Shortie. You the man, Willie! Big ups* to ya, MVP, old head of Tioga! Second Shortie. You the man Willie! Big ups to ya, old head of North Philly!

Third Shortie. You the man Willie! You'll be king of the hill from now on!

Hartie. Yo man, why do you look ready, and appear scared to words that ring honest? Sounds good to me. Are you really what you are, or really what you look like? Y'all confronted my boy with all this respect and wild prediction of taking over the top spot.

ups: respect.

He's now dreaming. However, you all ain't said nothing to me. If you can lean back and look deep into time, tell which flower will bloom and which will not. Talk to me, who doesn't whine or back down from your truths or lies.

First Shortie. Salute!

Second Shortie. Salute!

Third Shortie. Salute!

First Shortie.   Not as good as Willie, and better.

Second Shortie. Not so lucky, yet much luckier.

Third Shortie. You'll get players. Yet, you won't be none.

So big props* to Willie and Hartie!

First Shortie.   Hartie and Willie, the bomb ski... *

Willie.   Hold up, you talking wags, give me the 411.* By William's* demise I
                 know I'm

                 the star of the Mustangs,* but how the Most Valuable Player? The
                 Captain of the Mustangs still plays. He's hitting over six hundred, and to
                 approach that is not reasonable for me to believe. Let alone MVP. Tell
                 me, where do you all get such whack* information. Better yet, why did
                 y'all stop us in this vacant lot with this foretelling bull. Say something. I
                 demand you.

                 [Shorties get ghost.*]

Hartie.   Fog flouts over the earth, and heavier over water, and that's what they were.
                 Where did they go?

Willie.   They just vanished, seeming so live, into thin air. Just a few seconds and, oh
                 well.

*props: respect. bomb ski: slang, all that and a bag of chips. 411: information
(telephone number for operator assistance.) William's: Willie's dad. Mustangs:
famed baseball team from Philadelphia's Fairmount Park "A" League (Pa.) whack:
crazy. get ghost: slang, disappear.

Hartie.	Man did that just really happen? Or have we had too much sugar? You know it gets us souped.*
Willie.	Your kids will be players.
Hartie.	You will be an All-Star.
Willie.	And MVP too. Is it crazy?

[Enter JoJo and Larry.]

JoJo.	The Royal has heard how well you played, Willie, the no-hitter that you threw. And when he checks the box scores for how many strikeouts you had, he'll freak out. Not knowing whether to be in awe or kiss-up.* Plus, in analyzing this game day, he heard that you went into the heart of the Valley and just reared back and threw strikes, killing them. The word got back quickly. Everybody fessed up that you represented and had to bear witness to Bubba.
Larry.	We came or they told us to come, to give you a message of admiration, and to get you signed with the team. Not for peanuts!
JoJo.	And then a compliment of the highest degree, he told me to refer to you as the "League MVP". That's your title, you the man chief! It's yours.
Hartie.	Well I'll be... the fiends don't lie.
Willie.	The league MVP is live. Why do you drape me with zirconium bling?*
Larry.	You're right. Dude is still playing, but he doesn't deserve that title. I have reason to believe that he persuaded all pitchers to throw lollipops thus gaining the advantage. It's hard to prove. However, we'll step to him.
Willie.	[Aside] All-Star and MVP. The hard part's over. [To JoJo and Larry] good info. [to Hartie] you know one day your boys will be MVP too. I promise you, like me they're just as good.
Hartie.	I fully understand, this could swell your head, and make you think of

bigger things like ownership or the league's top spot. Those mangy wags told us truths, made us think about the possibilities. Homey, let me rap to you.

Willie.   [Aside] Two true happenings are playing out nicely. The tuna will be king.

souped: charged up. kiss-up: brown nosing. zirconium bling: fake diamonds.

Yo, thanks a lot y'all.

[aside]   Those predictions... I'm sold, they can't be wrong. I'm already feeling the power. I am the League MVP. It's easy for me to say it. I don't feel anything wrong. The thought seems natural. What, am I scared of this thought to expose Him...Fantastic! In my mind it's all right, and it is what it is!

Hartie.   The boys really like it see.

Willie.   [aside] If things fall into place, I'll be the man without even doing anything.

Hartie.   Everything's happening so fast... so new…hang not onto every word. Look out now!

Willie.   What will be, will be. You have to go through twenty-four hours, even on tough days.

Hartie.   Yo Willie, anytime you're ready.

Willie.   My bad…my mind's caught up in some things. Aw, forget it. I can feel you…every day is a new day. Come on let's go to the game.

[to Hartie] Think about what's happened…it's deep, and let's talk openly about it with each other.

Hartie.   I'm down.

Willie.   Later gator. Come on amigos.   [Exit.]

SCENE 4

[Fairmount Park. Fans cheer. Enter Ernie, Monty, Tony, Clyde and other Players]

Ernie.   Are them boys run out of Tioga? Did our boys get back yet?

Monty.   Yo big dog,* They didn't get back yet, but I talked with somebody that
said they got slaughtered. Their runner was fessing up for trying to take
over. I mean he was really sorry. Nothing was sweeter than to see him
get his tail whooped! He went back to the Valley disgraced, no longer
the runner. He blew that.

Ernie.   You never know about people... we use to be boys in school.

                    [Enter Willie, Hartie, JoJo, and Larry.]

              Yo man, you guys are it. Even that compliment isn't enough. I owe you
all more than you all can imagine.

              *Yo... dog: head man.

Willie.	Don't worry about it, it will take care of itself. Besides, we owe it to you, our leader. We're team players... we got your back.
Ernie.	Good show. I'm going to put you up, and make sure that the air keeps you high and rare. Big Hartie, you should be on the same level. So, let me tell you, I'm going to square things with you too.
Hartie.	Whatever I have, it's all good for the family.*
Ernie.	That really makes me feel good. A lot of people would be just faking. Yo, everybody, all y'all hear me now, I want to be up front about it. Skippy (Monty) will take over Tioga in the near future. Respect him and be proper like. He's the next runner to keep us together.
Willie.	Okay then, you say he's the man, then he's the man. I'll be the first to spread the good news. Let me go tell my girl...I'll catch you later... easy on.*
Ernie.	Yo, Big Skip... Runner!
Willie.	[aside] The Runner of Tioga! That means, the best that I can do is second, or leapfrog. He's in the way of what I want, but, let me just chill. I'll be cool and wait for the right moment, then move. It'll be like greased lightening when it's all over.
Ernie.	Dam, Willie took that well. I'm satisfied. So, let's have a party. He's gone but let's to his spot, where I know we're welcomed. He's a cool dude

SCENE 5

[Sugar Shack. Willie's pad. Enter his girl Goldie reading]

Goldie.	They came upon me on a day of prosperity, and I found out by the exact knowledge, they had more information than you could imagine. They performed some kind of magic and faded into the fog. My mouth was wide open, it was impressive. Some dudes came from the Sovereignty

and called me, the - Most Valuable Player- and that's the same title that the three Shorties had given me, and said that it would happen in due time, with "Big Daddy, MVP you shall be"! I thought that the best thing would be to tell you, my Honey Bunny, so that you would not be lacking in the party, by not knowing what an awesome promise is in there for you. Keep it on the down low,* rap to you later.

My Old Head, you already are, and now, MVP shall you be, just as assured. However, I'm not confident in your personality. You have within, gallons of the juice of man's compassion.

*family: not kinship...loyalty. easy on: take care. down low: secret.

To capitalize in this quickly this would make you great. You're not without desire but lack the deviance that has to be with it too. The demonic should also be in the mix. What you would is held highly, what you would is spiritual - would you not play fake for it?

And would that be unfair if you won? What's duly yours Big Daddy, screams out "you gotta do, what you gotta do" to get what you want. Some you're scared to deal, but I promise that once you do, you'll not regret the" didn't do." Come to me now, so that I can sweeten you with my sugars in your brain, so that I can castigate you with the penetration of my eyes, everything that prohibits you from the ice diamond* which the stars and the supernatural seem to unquestionably lay at your feet.

[Enter a Bearer]   What you got?

Bearer. Ernie is coming to the crib tonight.

Goldie. Wow! You are sick* with words. Is the ruler of the house with him? Who, if it's true, would have clued me in for some preparation.

Bearer. I see you glowing, sho* you right; our Main Man is coming. One of his boys ran ahead of him, arriving all out of breath and half dead, and could barely deliver the message.

Goldie. Lay something on him... a few bucks, this news is great.

[Exit Bearer]

The hell hounds howl that signal the fateful arrival of Ernie with me at the helm. Come animus* into me that feed on human schemes, relieve me of feminine sex, and top off my tank with the worst inhumanity! Stretch out my talons, shut off every entrance for softness, so that nothing of pity or nature's regret can penetrate, erupt my eternal fate not allowing sanity around the act and it! Invade into my woman's feed*, and extract the leche* for acerb*, you homicide holy's, whenever in thou mindless natures, you patience with natural misconduct! Here heavy night, and draw me in the darkest shade of Hades, so my blade is not aware of the cut it inflicts, not letting Angels see through the quilt of the night to bellow "Maintain Maintain!"

[Enter Willie]

Oh, All-Star! Great MVP! Even better than both, by the all-trumpet afterlife! Your scripts have transplanted me further than this unknowledgeable instant, and I enveloped ahora*, the hereafter in the moment.

Willie. My sweet baby, Ernie arrives here tonight.

Goldie. How long is his stay?

*ice diamond: crown. sick: crazy. sho: (slang) sure. animus: spirits. feed: breast. leche: milk. acerb: bitterness.ahora: now.

Willie. He completes his mission by tomorrow.

Goldie. Well, he'll never get out of here seeing the sun! Your kisser, my Great, is like a video where dancers do strange gyrations. To bamboozle the time, play the · part of time, let your eyes show warmth, your body language, your speech. Look like the gentle wave but be the riptide underneath. Him that's arriving has to be made comfortable, and you just leave this good nightly order up to me. This will decorate all of our days and nights forever. Show your power and master the night.

Willie. We'll rap more.

Goldie. Show only your angelic. To switch look, is even to scare. I'll handle it.

SCENE 6

[At Willie's pad. Clarinets and search lights. Enter Ernie, Monty, Tony, Hartie, Clyde, Dawson, JoJo, Larry and the crew.]

Ernie. This stadium is in quite a nice spot. The freshly cut grass is sweet and brings out the energy in my body.

Hartie. It's ready for summer. The cardinal flies about and does approve. I like the way it is built, that has a celestial air, with scents of coziness about. No overhanging decks, lack of support, nor unlighted corners. The house bird has made a comfortable nest where rookies can be spawned and nurtured. This, where all the game takes place, I can see that the air is rare.

[Enter Goldie]

Ernie. Here, here our loyal mistress of ceremony! Your graciousness that trails us, sometimes puts us through trouble. Yet, we thank you with love, knowing that the Lord will reward you for your effort and humble us for your trouble.

Goldie. Every amenity has been touched, and retouched again and again ... that's cuatro veces,* the slight business that contends pales against the deep and wide honors that you've brought within. Take full advantage of our house my king. As did many of importance have from days of old, our prayers are of pastors.*

Ernie. Where's the MVP. We were hotly behind him hoping that we would precede him and have everything already laid out. However, he was on his Harley-Davidson which he rides well, and that love and crisp of ride has helped him,

cuatro veces: four times. pastors: we pray the prayers of pastors.

to get here ahead of us. Beautiful woman we are intrigued... you are our hostess tonight.

Goldie. Your servants for life, have them, all of them at your disposal. To perform their accounts at and for your majesty most fun. Eternal to you.

Ernie. Take my head and lead me to my master of ceremony. We are truly charmed by him and will see to reward him even more. I follow your footsteps, hostess.

SCENE 7

[Willie's crib. Enter maids and butlers with trays of food and silverware. Then, enters Willie.]

Willie. I just want to do this thing and get it over with. If this take down could only be done without any problems, then I could go on running things successfully. This knockoff would be the mother of all knockoffs here and now... final. However, right now in this space of time it is a risk to what follows. But in times like these, we still control things here, I know that what you send out oftentimes, returns to catch the sender. This symmetry in-equitableness mirrors the look of our rotten plate with food for our own mouths. He stays under a double faith. Number one, he's the owner and I play for him, those two make me have second thoughts. Also, he is my company who I should bar the door against any harm coming his way, not use the gun on him myself. Additionally, Ernie has been a great owner... he pays, and his office is always accessible. His fairness with people will set off sirens and outrage against him being eliminated. It will be like striking an innocent fawn, and beautiful maidens will carry this unkind deed across all the waters. And in every heart the beat will darken the sun. Yet, there is no sign to show me retreat, only my greed, and lust for power overtakes me (who I am) and lets in no good on the other side.

[Enter Goldie]

My dear! What is happening?

Goldie. He is just about finished eating. Why did you leave the great room?

Willie. Did he ask where I was?

Goldie. Don't you know this, yes?

Willie. I do not want this thing to carry on any further. I just got a new contract from him, which all the pressBand people know is outstanding, I want to bask in that new sun rise, not just throw it to the wind so quickly.

Goldie. Was your dream drugged where you envisioned yourself? Are you sleeping now, only to awaken so yellow, afraid and frightened at what you know is the thing that's freeing? Right here, and right now, I inventory your love. Are you scared to do with fortitude what you dream of? Don't you want that trophy which can validate your life not being cowardly towards your own dreams? Entertaining…I "shoulda," "woulda," "coulda," like the old adage "play ball, but don't get dirty."

Willie. Woman please, and peace. I don't have to do anything to prove I am a man. I do it all.

Goldie. What was the monster that bade you show this business to me? Not only most valuable player, buy owner too! You'd be more than a player. No time or place is suitable, but you will deal with both, this is what's presented, and the opportunity here does define you. My hips do form and sway with tender for the birth of the loving baby. I will upon seeing its newborn face, snatch it from my vagina naked and hurling downward broken bones, if I had promised to do so, as you have promised to see this through.

Willie. What if we get caught?

Goldie. We default! Only attach your mind to the objective, and there's no problem. When Ernie is sleeping- you know, after his long hard day, and Mr. Sandman overtakes him... then will I with his boy's impart riotous getting high of smoking and drinking ... they'll be so, pickled that their thoughts and memory will be mush, and their understandings will be that of a baby. They will be stretched out in a sedated state like being dead. At that point, we can do what we want, do, anything to Ernie. His boys of a stupor, will get the blame of our taking him out.*

Willie. Call up the man-child, your vigor and strength of spirit to do this well, is like that of men. It will appear when we have poison* injected his body with holes, done by the sleepy friends of his room, and using their own works* to do the job.

Goldie. How can it be seen any other way? We will act distraught, and wail against his demise.

Willie. Yo, that's the plan, I'm down* with it. Let's both haul tail until the time as such must take place. Deceived mind must cover what the deceived soul does know.

*out: murder. poison: drug. works: needles. down: ok.

ACT TWO: THE GAME

SCENE 1

[Diamond # 1 Mustangs home field. Enter Hartie, and Norman holding flashlight.]

Hartie. What's going on, young fellow?

Norman. It's dark as hell. . .I have no idea what time it is.

Hartie. Looks to be around midnight.

Norman. Might be a little later, dad.

Hartie. Here, hold my bat. I wish I had a dollar for every star in the universe. It would
   be lights out. Here, hold my glove, my spikes too. This equipment is heavy and
   wears me out. I can't really catch any Z's.* Thankfully, forces hold me back
   from vicious thoughts that nature brings when I'm in a state of rest.

[Enter Willie and a friend with a flashlight.]

Yo! Give me my bat. Who comes?

Willie. It's your boy.

Hartie. Yo man, you ain't crashed yet? The Sovereign is racked.* He was feeling kinda

sporty... and was giving away "C" * notes to the boys. The jewel he served your lady in

addition, called her the best entertainer, and then eased to his room smiling all the way.

Willie. We were not really ready, we rushed, and I know everything wasn't right.

Things could have been better if we had more heads up.*

Hartie. I had a dream about those three Shorties last night. For you, they seem to be
   straight butter.*

Willie. Man, I ain't thinking about those enchantresses. However, when you have a few

minutes to spend, we would be availed in some rap concerning some business. If you

have the time.

Hartie. No problem ... whenever you're ready.

*Z's: sleep. racked: in bed. "C" notes: a one hundred bill. heads up: advanced notice. straight butter: the truth be said.

Willie. Yo, if you dummy up* to what's happening, there're some bennies* in it for you.

Hartie. Ah, so long as there's no skin off my nose for helping, and my head is limpid in the sovereign's corner. Bring it... what you got I say?

Willie. Beautiful, go rest up a while!

Hartie. Yo bro. Backatcha!

[Exit Hartie and Norman.]

Willie. Go tell my baby, to roll me a smoke,[Exit Friend.] and put on some sweet music. You go crash. Is this a syringe that I envision, the plunger caressing my thumb. Here, here, I'll grab it. It's not actual, but it is there. Are my eyes deceived of this real matter, to touch as to see? Or is this just a figment of my imagination, a phony baloney, forwarding from my stressed-out mind? I envision it yet, so clearly as this thing that now I possess. It takes me in the direction that I was headed; And this tool that I must use. My eyes are playing tricks e' the other five, or else equal to all the like. There it is again, and on the needle and plunger drops of boy* not splashed before. This can't be. Yes, this wicked activity is engaged, fit into my sight. Here only half the world seems alive, and dreams are robbed of their pleasant nature of sleep. Devilment parties Heathercat's* contributions, plus tattered killing, alerted by his guard, the pit bull, who keeps clock by his growl... to the extent of his furtive motion, with Jesse's eloquent lopes,* forward this project streaming like a disembodied soul. My feet are firmly planted, as I go tipping down the walkway, scared that the blowing leaves speak of my local, and takes midnight here and now, to the situation thus called. As I plot, he exists. Thoughts to the hot of the deed to chilling to exhale. I sprint and it's over. The drum calls me. [a drumbeat] Deaf to you Ernie, because it is the rhythm that calls you to paradise or poison.

SCENE 2

[The identical. Enter Goldie.]

Goldie. That which has made me high has made me cocky. What has mellowed them, has given me storm. Hark! Quiet! It is the wolf that wails the cry of the determined hunter, that yields the still of the night. That man is bout it, bout it.* Walk right on in, the stuffed defenders* have abandoned their posts for sleep. I have laced their herbs. That they do not know what impetus is about them. Whether they sink or swim.

*dummy up: play along. bennies: Benjamin Franklin who's on the 20-dollar bill. e': same purpose as o' connective vowel boy: heroin. Heathercat: goddess of trickery ... to whom the shorties are allied. Jesse's...lopes: Jesse Owens Olympic champion. bout it, bout it: of doing the deed. defenders: protectors of the sovereign.

Willie. [within] What the? Yo, ho!

Goldie. Damn, I'm tripping, they arise, and it's not even happened. The effort and not the act is what will doom us. I've placed the syringes to the ready, he had to see them. If he didn't look like my step while sleeping, I could have bumped him off.

[Enter Willie.]   My spouse!

Willie. I've taken care of business. To you, was everything not mouse?*

Goldie. I heard the pit growl and the snake rattle. Did you say something?

Willie. At what time?

Goldie. Presently.

Willie. When I came down?

Goldie. Yeah.

Willie. Listen! Who sleeps in bedroom number two?

Goldie. His son, Tony.

Willie. This picture is wacked!*   [looking at his hands.]

Goldie. Don't start going out on me, by saying wacked picture.

Willie. One started giggling in his sleep, and one shouted "O-D!"* It's a wonder that they didn't wake each other up. I heard them, they were of invocation, and quickly fell back to sleep.

Goldie. Two are sleeping on the couch.

Willie. One said, "Jesus Wept!" and" Sho nuff,"* his boy, they were half awake and saw my poisonous claws Taking in their scares, I couldn't utter "that's right" When they did say "Jesus Wept!"

Goldie. Shake it off ... don't dwell on it.

*mouse: quiet, (not mouse) ... not noisy. wacked: crazy "0-D'": drug overdose. "Sho nuff': correct.

Willie. But you know, I couldn't get my words out "Sho nuff." I really needed

something divine, and "Sho nuff just caught in the pipes.

Goldie. Put the matter out cha* mind. After what went down, it will drive us crazy.

Willie. I could have sworn that someone shouted, "Slumber no more! Willie did o-d

slumber" the pure slumber. Slumber that sooths a hectic day - ah good slumber...

the station at the end of each day's travel, tired feet's relief, remedy to the aching

heart, the Giver's other half. The wine that toasts this world.

Goldie: What's that you say?

Willie. It continued to shout, "Slumber no more!" en toda la casa.* "Southern* hath

lullabied* slumber, consequently, the MVP will slumber never again. Willie will

never again slumber."

Goldie. Who was it that shouts? The reason, valued champ, you must unwind, your

blue-blooded power to contemplate such cerebral ill things. Yo, get some

alcohol, and clean that dirty evidence from your extremities. Why do you bring

these works from there? They should have stayed. Take them back and sprinkle

the caretakers with "boy"*

Willie. I ain't. I'm too scared to even imagine what I did. Think about it more, I don't

think so.

Goldie. Brother be strong! Give me those spikes. The slumbering and the demised ain't

nutt'n but snap shots. It's the face of a baby, that alarms at Godzilla. If he does

foam, I'll foam the lips of his boys too. For true, they'll look guilty.

[Exit Chimes inside.]

Willie. Where is that chime coming from? Why does every little sound rattler* me?

What fists have come?

Yo, they knock me out cold! Will Zeus's great mountains overshadow this

powder blowing it from my hands? Not, this hand of mine will instead the

majestic mountain blizzards, turning the white one black.

[Reenter Goldie.]

Goldie.My hands are powdered like yours, but I counterfeit to have a mind so clear. [Chimes inside.] I hear the chimes at the back door. Recede to our racks. A little fan exchanges us from the crime. It will be much smoother to stick to the plan. Have you already gone without me? [Chimes inside.] Attention! More chimes.

cha: your. en...casa: in all the house. Southern: South Phila. High School., Willie's alma mater. lullabied: killed. boy: (slang) heroin. rattler: is like a snake and rattles the soul.

Put on your jammies,* so the situation won't bring us forth to be partakers. And don't start that bawling!

Willie. To think about what I've done, it's better not to know my mind. [Chimes inside.] Arise Ernie with the chimes! I could if you wouldst! [Exit.]

SCENE 3

[The identical. Enter a Bellhop. Chimes within.]

Bellhop. Yes, I do hear a chime actually! If a person were a bellhop at the Peachtree,* he should catch young, admitting the lovers. [Chimes inside.] Yo yo yooo! What's up, me, the name is Angel. I know a girl so ugly, she had to sneak-up on a glass of water. [Chimes inside.] Yo, yo! What's up for heaven sakes. Your momma is so dumb, she thought a quarterback was a refund. Oh, it's like that, talking about my momma! [Chimes inside.] Ho, ho, hooo! What's up, now? Why did the moron take a ladder to the baseball game? Why? Because he heard the Giants were playing. [Chimes inside.] Yo, yo, things are hectic! What the hey! It's too hot to be paradise. I'll heavenly- bellhop no more. For me, it's ushering up all lifestyles to the sugar shack* way of lifelong bliss. [Chimes within.] Alas, alas, I hope you don't forget about the bellhop.

[Raises the shutters.]

[Enter Dawson and Clyde.]

Dawson. Wake up chump, you sleep already? Is it that late?

Bellhop. Chill man, we were tote'n* till four clocks, and the plant gets you going with trio the stimulations.

Dawson. What kind of trio stimulation does reefer bring about?

Bellhop. Funny wisdom sir, I believe they call it being heavy. * Hunger or munchies. Nympho man, it stimulates and super stimulates. It stimulates the drive and enhances the power. Thus, good smoke is thought to be the equivalent to oyster. It takes him, and it makes him. It turns him on and turns him up. It seduces you, then juices you. It makes him stand hard and stand rubbery. It equalizes him in dreams and provides the word, then vanishes.

Dawson. I know smoking gives you the word this night.

Bellhop. Sho you right man, the very voice in me. Yet, I resisted it for the word, and I thought I was being strong. But it grabbed my head and spun it around.

*jammies: pajamas. Peachtree: hotel in Atlanta Ga. Sugar shack: house of love. tote'n: smoking herb. heavy: overly poetic, intelligent.

However, I got some fresh air to wake myself.

Dawson. Is the MVP moving about?

[Enter Willie.]

The chimes have gotten him up There's the brother now.

Clyde. Good morning Bro.

Willie. Yeah, back at you all.

Dawson. Is Ernie moving around anywhere player/player*?

Willie.   No sir.

Dawson. He asked me to stop by this morning, it almost slipped my mind.

Willie. Follow me, I'll take you there.

Dawson. I can see that you're grooving off of this hassle, but it still is a bothersome thing.

Willie. This kind of work is good for us. Here is the room.

Dawson. Thanks, I'll wake him up... that's about all the job I'll have to do today.

[Exit.]

Clyde. Is he leaving for a Combine* today?

Willie. Yeah, it's on this schedule.

[Schedule on the refrigerator.]

Clyde. It's been a crazy night around town. The roofs came off, and truth be told, I
heard the fluttering weird hollering of murder, and predicting utters of straight
lunacy, and shear madness. Hatching newmto this wretched period. The rat-
bird* screeched the short dead night. Many believe the third rock from
the sun was vomiting and likely convulsed.

Willie. It was a hellish night.

Clyde. I can't liken anything to it throughout my juvenile life.

[Reenter Dawson.]

*player/player: cool dude. Combine: camp where new players are evaluated. rat-bird: bat.

Dawson. Oh, hell no, hell no! Mind nor soul will not imagine or put it into words!

Willie. What's the matter?

Clyde. What's the matter?

Dawson. Helter-skelter today has poured his supreme. Consecrated death has invaded
the team's top spot and vanquished the essence of the palace!

Willie. What you talkin' bout? The essence?

Clyde. You saying the Boss?

Dawson. Check the bedroom, and blind yourself, ten times the Komodo Dragon. Look,
then tell words o' the second person. *

[Exit Willie and Clyde.]

Arise, arise! Sound the base drum. Death and betrayal! Hartie and Tony!
Monty! Arise! Slide out your slumber, dreams legitimate, and look upon
horror's image. Rise, rise and read the awesome final chapter! * Skippy! Hartie!
Like from your deep six rack* escape, and move like supernaturals,
to compose this madness, Sound the Chimes.

[Enter Goldie.]

Goldie. What's going on, that such a disastrous voice summons together those who are
slumbering within this house? Well, tell!

Dawson. Oh mild woman, what I have to say, must not be heard by you. The reiteration in
a lady's mind could stifle as it sounds.

[Enter Hartie.]

Oh Hartie, Hartie! The ball club's owner is iced. *

Goldie. What the hell! Here, in this crib... ours!

Hartie. No leniency about. My Daw, I pray thee! Be opposite of what you say. Tell me
it's a lie.

[Reenter Willie and Clyde with JoJo.]

Willie. Had I been born a minute after this event, I would have lived my days in a
glorious span, because from this moment everything' s joyous of immortality.
All is our playthings. * Fame and greatness would not live, the butter from the
duck has been gotten, and what's left, is for history to sing of.

*second person: ref. to speech ... you, yourself speak. final chapter: book of life... the
end. deep... rack: graves dug six feet down. iced: slang ... killed. playthings: toys.

[Enter Skip and Tony.]

Tony. What's the problem?

Willie. You ascend but are mindless of it. The dome, the peak, the apex of your existence
    is chopped.

Dawson. The life of your great dad, has been had.

Skip. Really, who did it?

Clyde. It appears that people in this pad did it. Their looks are nervous, and there's dust
    in their eyes... not to mention their needle filled clothes, that were found powder
    marked in the hamper. They are shaken and disheveled. No male should've
    entrusted their existence to them.

Willie. Wow, I do regret myself for my rage of, I have destroyed those, ... those.

Dawson. Can you explain yourself?

Willie. What can be steady, tempest, mild and spicy, faithful, and in between, all at
    once? No male. The quick journey of my obsessed love speeds beyond the
    restraint of better judgement. See who lays here,
    Ernie! His fragile body pricked by heroin's point, and his lifeless veins appear
    like a motionless river in nature from source mouth. Here, the killers mired in
    the soil of their business. Their syringes with dirty points and drips can any
    hold back, that has a passion to love, and in that passion, the strength to
    make that love accessed?

Goldie. Help me from this point, Boo! *

Dawson. Secure the Honey. *

Monty/Skip. [Aside to Tony] For what reason do we sow silence into our mouth's,
    when everyone may allege that this outrage is ours?

Tony. [Aside to Skip] We'll not seal our fate by speaking here with minute words
    spoken, to be overpowered, and have grasp inflicted upon us. Let's just haul ass.
    Our winds are not yet a hurricane.

Monty/Skip. [Aside to Tony] Neither our powerful grief has started to generate.

Boo: affectionate ref. to one's mate, significant other or spouse. Honey: lady, girl, female.

Hartie. Eyes to the lady.

[Goldie is stretchered off.]

And when we cover our exposed weaknesses that are exhausted by sight, we will meet again and analyze this most needled act of incidence, to understand it more. Scares and backstabbers tremble us.

In the paw of the Almighty am I, and from this time opposing the hidden agenda I do battle the deliberate betrayal of trust, yet not known.

Dawson. Likewise, I'm sure.

All.   Yeah boy!

Willie. We can quickly jump into our gorilla suits, * and join me at the club everyone.

All. At the club.

[Exit all but Skip and Tony.]

Skip.   Yo bro, what cha know'? We can't hang out with these clowns. To reveal a fake "a" caring is a room that

the untrue guy decorates with lax. I'm going to the Big Apple. *

Tony. Me, S. B.* Yeah. The opposite paths will keep us from harm's way. Because here, there are syringes in the laughs of every man. We are direct descendants, which makes us more directly deceased.

Skip. This sinister spear that's hurled has not flaked yet, so best we get to stepp'n so it can miss the mark. What I'm saying is, "jump into your ride, and don't be shy about splitting the scene. Steal away. There's justification in the robbery, that robs itself when all sympathy is gone."

SCENE 4

[They leave.]

[Outside Willie's mansion. Enter JoJo with Old Man Jake.]

Jake. Back in Hoover's* day, seems like just yesterday. I've seen many a harsh hour in my span, dirty times and weird times too. But what has happened this night, makes those things look like baked cookies.

JoJo. Yo daddy - O, you see even the Gods have trouble with this thing, intimidating their arena con sangre. * By my watch it's a.m. However, the blackened night chokes the journeying lantern. *

*gorilla suit: macho attitude. Big Apple: New York City. S. B: South Beach. Hoover's day: ref. to the depression during the term of pres. Herbert Hoover 1929-1933. con sangre: with blood. lantern: sun.

It' a got to be, night is dominating, or the day has given up. That blackness has swallowed up the earth,

yet, loving light should have smooched it?

Jake. It ain't right, just ain't right'. Just like what's happened. On Tiwesdaeg* of last week' an eagle soaring at its height of excellence was shadowed by this miniature falcon, zapped and terminated.

JoJo. And Ernie's cars-the weirdest and truest thing-gorgeous and powerful, the best cars and jeeps that money can buy. Without warning suddenly started, geared up and blew out the garage, unnatural,

unbelievable, unstoppable, like they were going to hook off on the hood (crash throughout the hood).

Jake. People say they all smashed into themselves.

JoJo. Correct, I witnessed it without believing what I was looking at. Here comes the high-grade Dawson.

[Enter Dawson.]

What's life like at this very minute?

Dawson. Can't you see yourself.

JoJo.   Nobody still does not know who did this terrible thing?

Dawson. Them boys that Willie took out. *

JoJo.   Oh, what a night! What alibi could they have given up?

Dawson. They said that they were paid. Skip and Tony from the sovereign's fountain,
        they skipped town. That makes them look suspect to the whole thing.

JoJo.   Yeah, that is contrary to the natural. Cheap hopes eaten so hungrily, your own
        family! Probably Mustang ownership will be passed on to Willie.

Dawson. It's already a done deal, he's on his way to the Downtown Athletic Club* to
        be vested.

JoJo.   Where is Ernie's carcass?

Dawson. Gone to Laurel Hill, * The cemetery right next to the baseball field, where
        you

*Tiwesdaeg: OE. Tuesday. took out: killed. Downtown Athletic Club: where great athletes
receive awards and trophies. Laurel Hill: famed burial grounds in Fairmount Park.

can see the before players and the resting place of their calcareous* house.

JoJo.   To the Piccadilly? *

Dawson. Nay to the Hamptons* for me.

JoJo.   Well, I guess it's to that place for me.

Dawson. Ok, I hope everything's cool there. Easy on Perhaps the devil we know, is better than the devil we don't know! *

JoJo.   Later old man.

Jake.   Deus Benedictus* follow you, and with any that orchestrates sugar from vinegar and buds* from duds.

*calcareous: bones. Piccadilly: exotic club for cuisine, dancers, where mustangs are celebrated.
Hamptons: Dawson's mansion. Perhaps…know: making reference to the Mustangs future under Willie. Deus Benedictus: Lords blessing. buds: buddies.

35

ACT THREE: SEVENTH INNING STRETCH

SCENE 1

[Fairmount Park. Diamond # 1. Enter Hartie.]

Hartie. It's your hill Will. Owner, manager, MVP... everything, just as the Shorties
   predicted, and I do believe that you got it by hook or crook. However, it is
   written, it should not affect my success, I know my history, that I am absorbed
   and should procure many rulers. If what they say comes true-as it did for
   you, Willie, their essays gleamed- How, but the realism on you good was made.
   Perhaps, they not be my journalists too! And build up me upon wishes? Peace
   be still.

[Drum roll. Enter Willie as owner, Goldie, as his spouse; Clyde, JoJo, Ballplayers,
Females, and Helpers.]

Willie. Here is our most hospitable person.
Goldie. If he had been shunned ... something would be missed at our special party and
certainly distasteful.
Willie. Today's night is when we have our formal dinner, I beg that your presence be
   there.

Hartie. Your greatness has control over me, through which my dedication is

      unquestionably woven and spread forever.

Willie. Do you have to make a midday run?

Hartie. Yes sir buddy.

Willie. Two are in want of your wise recommendation that ultimately has been positive

      and negative, in this day's events, however, we will get to that manana. * Do

      you have to roll a distance?

Hartie. About as far as it will take to get back here for the dinner. Just as fast as my

      motorcycle or better I'll fly. I'll have to take lend from the nocturnal. If not, I'll

      be late by an hour or two.

Willie. Don't stand us up for dinner.

Hartie. I'll be back, Jack.

Willie. The word is that the family is also held up in Jamaica and the Bahamas, lying

      about their vindictive parent-a-cide, * blistering any listener with weird device.

      Think of that in the next twenty and four when we will have reason of diplomat

      that will require our full state. Jet to your wheels. Later, till you come

      back to- night. Your son, Stormin Norman -will be with you?

Hartie. Yes sir. Look at the time, I've gotta split and take care of business.

Willie. I hope your bike runs like a swift footed jaguar. Thus, I do implant you behind

      the wheel. Adios amigo. Every person must control their own clock. Until eight

      tonight. To allow blue blood* to create the atmosphere of a fresher receiver.

      We'll tighten up till dinner* solo. Till then, peace and blessings be with to you!

[Exit everyone except Willie and a bodyguard.]

   Bleu, let me holla at you. Dig those dudes over there our happiness?

Man.   Yeah boss, they're just chill'n across from the park.

Willie. Bring um out. * Being the royal is bogus, unless you're to be a secured royal.

[Exit Man.]

manana: esp. tomorrow. parent-a-cide: (new word), killers of one's parents or, one's grandparents. blue blood: high society. tighten...dinner: stay in check. bring um out: slang, ... bring to me.

All apprehension is with Hartie, it is strong, caused by his wise old nature. His regal in the natural should be feared. He figures a lot, add that to the fearlessness of his clever mind. He's smart, and that steers his bravery. I must move cautiously. He's the only person that I do fear could contend. Next to him my cleverness is stifled, so they say Bigger's* was by the man. He scolded the Shorties when they primarily thrust MVP on me and prodded them to speak to him. Then parable like they extolled him padre to a host of MVP's. Atop my dome* they put a seedless wreath also, placing a melting baton within my fingers, and from that point to be plagued by a non-ancestral highway, no seed of mine ascending. If it's to be true, oh Hartie's controversy I have raped my mind, for them the noble Ernie I've killed, pouring spite in the cup of my tranquility. Exclusive for those and my infinite diamond* falling victim to the fallen angel of humankind, installing them mvp's the fruits of Hartie's rulers! Fairly than that, leap destiny, within the catalogue and challenge me to the shout! Who dat!

[Reenter Valet, with a couple of Killers.]

[Exit Valet.]

Yo bro, go watch the door till I send for you. I just spoke to you all the past twenty and four correct?

First Killer. Yeah, with all smiles your Sovereignty.

Willie. Okay then, are you in agreement with my essays? Realize that it was big "H"* all along that placed you under misfortune, which you thought was pure fate. I hyped* you to this at our former meeting and showed you how you were deceived all along by soured horns that blew all poor notes of a dim-witted mind... yeah, this by Hartie

First Killer. You were clear with it to us.

Willie. True I was, and even beyond which, will now be the focus of this follow up
      session. Is your calm so compelling to your make up, that you can just disperse
      this thing? Are you so spiritual as to entreat this hombre for his controversy?
      His fist has wriggled you to your crypt and left yours pleading eternally.

First Killer. We are male, my superior.

Willie. Yeah, in the dictionary you do translate male, as Siamese and Persians, tabby,
      Garfield, * domestic mouser's, and bobcats are classified. Each by the term of
      cat, their worth labeled, separating the rare, the exotic, the common, the funny,
      the house, and the killer, all based on the talent that awesome forces has set to

*Bigger: ref. to Langston Hughes character Bigger Thomas from novel Native Son.
dome: head. infinite diamond: eternal soul. "H": Hartie. hyped: made known to.
Garfield: cartoon cat.

them. Heretofore he does deserve special attention from the definition that links their
commonality. And thus of males. Now, do you have a spot in the line-up? It's not the
worst position for me to be, would you speak it, and I'll breath that issue into your
chest whose demise gets rid of your adversary, grips you to el corazon, y amor de
ambos. * Who renders our health ill as he lives, which otherwise by his death would be
el perfecto.

Second Killer. I'm on the same page my superior, where the vicious punches and slaps
          of the earth, make me so, outraged therefore, I am wanton in what I seek
          to malice this earth.

First Killer. Hey, I feel you... so tired with twisted mishaps, jerked with luck, that I'm
          ready to course another existence on any current that would success it or be
          gone of it.

Willie. Two together, you do acknowledge Hartie was your nemesis?

Both Killers. Yes Sahib.

Willie. True to me too; and in a bloody argument so as every hour of him being jammed amongst my very soul wishing that I could with absolute strength mop him

from my vision and would be able to justify it. However, I can't, because our like teammates of certain mind, whose love I couldn't let fall, however lament his drop that I alone struck out. * Thus, have I come by needing your services I do make whoopee*, hallucinating the deeds from the commoner for various heavy logics.

Second Killer. By us, if you say so boss, it is as good as done.

First Killer. Even if our lives-

Willie. Your dedications be heard within you. Through these minutes by many I will hip you where to seed yourselves. Be familiar yourselves with the smooth operation of the o'clock, the precise breath to do it. Let tonight be the night, and jetting from the compound*, me thinks that I must have all transparency. Thus, with heat leaving negative burns or bungles in the job- Stormin Norman his offspring that companions with him, with disappearance is not a bother to myself. Likened with his daddy should encircle the element of that pernicious hour. Do what you must. I'll inform you later.

Both Killers. Master, so let it be written, so let it be done!

*el corazon ... ambos: esp. the heart and love of both. struck out: assassinated. whoopee: to make love. compound: mansion

Willie. I'll come with request upon you directly... Stay secret. Now fade.

[Exit. Killers.]

It is straight. Hartie, your spirit's clout, should it locate Paradise, will locate it before this day is out!

[Exit.]

SCENE 2

[The compound. Enter Goldie and an Attendant.]

Goldie. Has Hartie left Joe's bar yet?

Attendant. Sho you're right, * however, he'll be back tonight.

Goldie. Tell the MVP I should desire him at his casual for some limited rap. *

Attendant. Madame, no problem.

Goldie. Nothing's had, everything's gone, where our wants are procured minus

       satisfaction. It's better to be secure with that which we demolish, than by

demolition thinketh in skeptical polish.

[Enter Willie.]

How bout it, my king! Why are you so all alone, borrowing the poor notions

that your company makes? Think not with them of those thoughts on going,

they should have expired, let them worry. Affairs that have no cure, should

have no concern. Hey, everything is everything.

Willie. We've just maimed the rottweiler, not eliminated it. He'll regenerate, and be his

      again, while my situation will remain in jeopardy as his previous coat.* Alas,

      things fall apart, and all of utopia would hurt, before we break bread scared and

      slumber in the disease of these horrible nightmares that plague us at stars.*

      Perhaps, it's better to be with the buried, whom we sought our freedom, having

      sent to freedom, rather than the torment on mind to remain in agony without

      heaven. Ernie is in his crypt, free from his fretful life and resting well. Betrayal

      having done its most awful. No guns, lethal injections, bad happenings, foul

      plots, nada can harm him anymore.

Goldie. Yo... hold steady big guy, shake off that tough face, be happy and party with your

sho you're right: slang...yes. limited rap: few words. in ... coat: still in peril like before. at stars: nighttime.

peeps* tonight.

Willie. I will do with affection and thus I entreat you. Put your focus to Hartie. Fall all over him lavish with smile and body language. We are not secure if we bathe our homage in this praising river, and Halloween our mugs to our heart, cloaking what they are.

Goldie. You have got to dismiss this.

Willie. Yea... filled with tarantulas is my brain, beloved spouse! You realize that Hartie and his Stormin' Norman are alive.

Goldie. For now, but not for long.

Willie. I am feeling better now because, they are vulnerable. Then now, be pleasant. before the snake has slithered his covered path, before dark Serpentina's call poison born fangs with numbing yawns, before dawn strips away the night, there will be a horrific act afloat.

Goldie. How shall we proceed?

Willie. Just be yourself, use ignorance of knowing, baby cakes, * until you clap the act. When the darkness falls, put away the sexy eyes of this dreadful day, and with great slaughter of unseen band, delete and dismember to nothing that giant cell, * that keeps me flush! "When morning comes, and the cows give milk to the world's wait, the happy times of day will wilt and fray. While sunlight keepers make their victims lay. You are amazed by my rap. Now stick and freeze, those misguided things started are made brawny themselves by sickness. Therefore, I beseech you, follow me.

[Exit.]

SCENE 3

[Fairmount Park 33rd & Dauphine (Mustang Stadium). Enter three Killers]

First Killer. Who gave you the holla to make a face* with us?

Third Killer. Willie.

Second Killer. He's cool, since he's ready to flow with what's going down line by line. *

*peeps: people. baby cakes: sweetheart. cell: Hartie's life. make a face: show up. line... line: detailed plan.

First Killer. Okay, you're in, no punk'n out! * The western sunrise stripes the new twenty-four; Yet hastens the delayed voyager winged footed. * profiting to house at just the right time, the person we are after.

Third Killer. Listen the sound of cycles. *

Hartie. [within] Shine the light here ho!

Second Killer. It's him, the others that will show at the banquet. I'm all ready for the stage.

First Killer. They are garaging his cycles.

Third Killer. It's just about one thousand, seven hundred and sixty yards; * that he normally-thus all dudes do-from here to home plate they take that walk.

Second Killer. Flashlight, flashlight!

[Enter Hartie and Stormin' Norman with a flare.]

Third Killer. That's him,

First Killer. Gear up.

Hartie. Gonna have showers this night.

First Killer. Handle your biz. *

[They move on Hartie.]

Hartie. O snap! * Haul "a"*- nice Norman, haul, haul, haul! That you may return for vengeance. O shackled one!

[Croaks. Norman decamps.]

Third Killer. Who turned out the bright?

First Killer. Wasn't it the thing?

Third Killer. Only one was taken out, his boy ran.

Second Killer. We have squandered the greatest portion of our plan.

First Killer. Hmmm, let us jet, and tell the part that's done.

[Exit.]

*punk'n out: getting scared and quitting. winged footed: fast a foot. cycles: motorcycles. one thousand, seven hundred and sixty yards: one mile. biz: business. Snap: what the hey! Haul "a": haul tail it.

SCENE 4

[Blue Horizon hall in the mansion. A feast readied. Coming in Willie, Goldie, JoJo, Clyde, Moons, and Stars.]

Willie. Everyone knows their average, * park it from top to bottom great greetings.

Moons. You the man!

Willie. Me myself and I, will flower amongst the crowd and play the low-key MC. Our chaperone maintains her royal spot, and in due time we'll bring her into the flow.

Goldie. Say it for me, daddy, to all our peeps, words from my breast, all are received.

[Enter First Killer, a la puerta.*]

Willie. Look, all meet us with appreciative minds. Every side is balanced. I'll remain in the atmosphere. Be jolly big, later we'll tip up a drink. * The round bar.

  [Nearing the entrance]. There's sangre* on your mug.

First Killer. Then it's Hartie's.

Willie. It's better off without him, then with him. Is he lullabied? *

First Killer. Big boy, his back is stabbed. I took care of it myself.

Willie. You are the best of the back stabbers. Tell me something good, that you did the mirror for Stormin Norman. If so, you are the man no question.

First Killer. Big guy, Stormin got away.

Willie. [Aside) Now my migraine, all over me repeated. Otherwise, I'd have been flawless, pure as the pearl, imbedded in the clam, as wide and free as the engulfing breeze. However, now I am housed, padded and locked, surrounded by uncertainties and scares. Safe however is Hartie.

First Killer. Yes sir! Big guy. Neatly tucked in a hole he continues, with ten deep cuts through his dome. * A less

    than natural death.

average: batting average... each seated according to his average. A 1a puerta: sp. door. tip... drink: toast. sangre: sp. blood. lullabied: put to sleep (death). dome: head.

Willie. I appreciate that.

[Aside] There the cultivated python rests. The garden snake, he's gone run away so that naturally in due time poison will beget, no jaws for now. Get the hell out of here, Manana* we'll listen and evaluate over again.

                                              [Exit Killers.]

Goldie. My kingly Boo, can you not play to the crowd? The banquet is just a meal, if you do not acknowledge your guest, while the festivities are happening. It's splurged with cheer. We can sup* well at the house. To go out, the elegance and the ambiance spices the meat. Parties are dull without it.

Willie. A good reminder! Now pleasant swallow serve on appetency, * and heartiness are the two.

Clyde. Your Grace if it pleases may I have seat?

        [The Spirit of Hartie enters and takes up residence in Willie's chair.]

Willie. The greatest players of our time are housed now. Yet, what of the noblest one of our feast Hartie, with time. I'd like to think that it's due to the chance that the thought was blown, rather than blown away by mischief. *

JoJo. The non-presence, boss, chalk it up to his pledge. Happier your king to join us with your good presence.

Willie. All places are taken.

Clyde. Here is a spot saved just for you.

Willie. Donde? *

Clyde. Aqui, * big daddy. What's making you stress Big Guy?

Willie. Yo, who's the wise guy?

Clyde. What you talkin' bout Sovereign?

Willie. You can't make me admit to being the architect. Don't sway those grandeur curls about me.

Manana: tomorrow (sp.). sup: eat (supper). appetency: appetite. I'd ... mischief: I hope he forgot rather than foul play. donde: where. aqui: here.

JoJo.   Players levantese! * The MVP is [falling down] losing it.

Goldie. Kizzy* good buddies. My man is sometimes this way, even from his days as a young boy. Bless you, remain with chair. This snap is but an instant, momentary thinking, He'll come back to the present with fitness.

If you stare on it too long, it bothers him and prolongs his fervor. Grub, and look not upon him. [to Willie] Are you the Master?

Willie. Yes, and a masterful one, who courageously looks at that which would even horrify Satan.

Goldie.   Damn good show!

This is just a figment of your imagination. It's just the wistful syringe that you said drew you to Ernie. Oh, these flashes that bring deceits to scare, shall translate to the child's tale at the campfire, sanctioned by the scout master. Be damned itself! Why do you taunt and wrinkle the mug? * After it's all finished, you appear just on a bench.

Willie. I pray, look, see! Egad! Oh snap! * What do you think of that? Yo, why should I worry? If you do not motion, make word also. If crypts and tombs of our caskets have to return those to whom we've laid to rest back, to our houses will be the scavenge of sharks.

[Exit Spirit.]

Goldie. What you are lacking, is your prudent good sense.

Willie. If I'm lying, I'm flying...I saw him.

Goldie. Really, oh disgrace!

Willie. The blood has been divested now, ah the old days, when lawlessness was the order, before marshals ruled. You know too, since those murders have taken place too troubling for the eye. The hour is thus that during the outing of the cerebellum, the man would expire, and that would be that. However, now they reincarnate, with tens of fatal killers on their wreaths, knocking us from the benches. This is even more fantastical than the killings.

Goldie. My true player. Your boys are missing you.

Willie. Yeah, I forgot, it slipped my mind. Hey y'all, don't mind me.

levantese: sp. raise up. Kizzy: from Roots, Kunta Kinte's daughter, means, stay put. mug: face. oh snap: slang, used to call attention to surprise.

I got this weird sickness, it isn't anything, at least to you all that know me. Let's party, peace and happiness to everybody, now I'll cop a spot. * So, tip up your cup and throw your hands up. I toast to the well-being of the whole dining, and to our beloved boy Hartie, who we would cherish if he were here! To everyone and him we guzzle, and everyone to everyone.

Players. Our commitments, and the promise.

[Spirit Returns.]

Willie. Haul "a"! * And duck from my eye! In the world be not visible! Your body is no skeleton, your muscles flat, you have no spark to perceive in that brain which you do concentrate with.

Goldie. Believe in this good player, just as something of tradition. It's trivial, it can only damage this hour of joy.

Willie. What soul challenge, I challenge. To draw near you like the vicious 'Hood pit,"* the night hidden panther, or the Tasmanian devil. Be any form but what it is, * thus my steady hands will not shake. Or return again to the living flesh and challenge us both to the tundra with my gat. * If afraid I'll remain indoors then, object me the infant of a boy. Jet* terrible shade! Superficial clone jet!

[Spirit disappears.]

Yes sirrrrrrr... Hauling "A".

I am a player once more. Heavens to you, remain seated.

Goldie. You have disheveled the joy, cracked the wonderful gathering, with highly marveled chaos.

Willie. Are these things possible, and able to be overruled like a winters frost, absent of our unique relationship? You have fashioned me foreign even to my own natural self. At this moment I believe you gaze upon this spectacle and maintain the natures balance of your body while mine is dizzy with fright.

JoJo. What scenes my Player?

Goldie. Have mercy and say nothing, he's sinking deeper and deeper. Preguntas* make him angry. Immediately, this is sayonara. * Don't rise according to protocol, but sayonara to all.

*cop a spot: sit down. Haul "a": begone. Hood pit: pitbull dog, breed made vicious in the neighborhood. Be...is: Hartie's form. gat: gun (slang). Jet: leave quickly. Preguntas: sp. questions. sayonara: goodbye. (Japanese).

Clyde. See you later, and I hope that you feel better. Look, take care of the MVP.

Goldie. Have a safe evening everybody!

[All leave but Willie and Goldie.]

Willie. They will have guts. Thus pronounced, guts will have guts. Mountains are believed to have shifted, and grass to mumble premonitions and things that are of significance. By flies cakes and pigeons and sparrows bring about the oozing of a man's guts. How goes the nightly?

Goldie. Nearly approaching the dawn with daylight, either is either.

Willie. Can it be explained, that Dawson refuses himself at our big party?

Goldie. Was word sent to him, man?

Willie. I heard it by and by, yet I will summon. I keep one of all of the help attached to my wallet as a snitch. I plan tomorrow, I will at times to the strange sibling's request that they tell more. Presently, I really need to construe if corrupt means the corrupt. For my own well-being, everything will fall apart. I am so far seeped in deep do-do* that I can stay afloat no more. Coming back is as shaky as going on. These chaotic thoughts in my brain will move my hand, which definitely will be played, or they'll be scrutinized.

Goldie. You're restless and need natures cure all, sleep.

Willie. Follow, we'll lie resting. My weird and self-attacks, is but an inexperienced fear that will better develop with time. The both of us are amateurs to these acts.

[Exit.]

SCENE 5

[A Pub. Steel Drums rumble. Appears the Three Shorties, confer with Heatherkat.]

First Shortie.   Yo! Sho you right, Heatherkat! You look swollen. *

Heatherkat. I guess so, scallywags hold fast, sassy and malapert. The audacity to mingle and mangle with Willie in rhymes and chimes of demise. Plus me, the h-m-i-c* of your magic, the unknown creator of all static, having not been summoned to partake in thus, nor reveal the honor of our artful bust? Also, which is more faulty, everything that you do, has been done for a wandering boo, * mean and irate, whom as some might have whoopee for his personal sum, never for your sight.

*do-do; excrement. swollen: angry. h-m-i-c: head mistress in charge. boo: man.

However, make things anew, now go jet silly, where, to invade the house of Piccadilly, * join me myself the day, the place, he will come to find what his future will be. Your bottles and your potions bring, your magic and all to spring. Thus, for me, the atmosphere this evening I shout, bring to a sad and bitter stop, "lights out." Charged matters have to be shaped by mid-day, upon the bundles of sun lit hay.

There pasted a dewy sun drop so plain, I will cradle it before it comes down as rain. And it pristinely by how sorcerer tricks it, will uproot the fake and wistful spirit. As by the power of the subline seduction, thus edging him closer to fatal destruction. Yes, he will reject destiny, loathe death, and their place, man's desires over knowledge, calm and disgrace. Surly you all realize that protection, is mortalities number one deception.

[Music and lyrics "Fly Robin Fly" etc.]

Listen! I am summoned. My tiny soul, view,

lays in a misty fog, awaiting me too.

[Exit.]

First Shortie. Over here, let us be in a rush, it's plain, she's due to make appearance again.

[Exeunt.]

SCENE 6

[Fairmount. The Park Mansion. Enter Clyde and another Head.]

Clyde. From what I was telling you before, has it hit you yet. By which you can figure out for yourself. I can only utter that affairs have been weirdly brought to life. The noble Ernie was sympathetic of Willie. Surprise he is killed. Also, the righteous - brave Hartie strolled too deep into the night. I guess it's said if you want the pleasure, Stormin Norman killed, because Norman skipped town. Males cannot stroll too far into the night. Is there anyone who can't imagine the idea how beastly it was for Monty and Tony to murder their stately old man? Damned true fact! Oh, how it did mourn Willie! Did not he directly in devout outrage, the failures rip that they were the victims of winery and servitudes to zzz's. * Wasn't that handled well? Yeahy, yeahyee, and artfully too. Yes, there should have been beef* by anybody living, for listening to those boys lie about it. Therefore, I speak to pronounce. He's done everything nobly. And I also believe that if he had Ernie's sons under lock- like it makes Heaven happy, that he doesn't-those boys

*Piccadilly: strip club of ill repute. zzz's: sleep. beef: anger issues.

would really discover what it means to terminate your pops. So would Stormin Norman. However, tranquility! From loose language phrases, and in edition he bombed, * his attendance at the dictator's dinner party. I understand that Dawson resides in shame. Brother, will you inform the whereabouts of his keep?

Lord Bethea. The offspring of Ernie, his birthright is being stymied by the dictator,
                 lives in the Venango Hall, and is embellished by the truly devout LaBoo
                 with great honor. Such that the vicious bad luck has done nothing to
                 tarnish his overall respect. Not to mention that Dawson has gone to
                 incorporate
The Giants* and fiery Jello, that with their assistance, and with the Creator to sanction the effort, there may be peace in the valley putting chow and grub before us, holy sleep to our midnights, released from parties and nightclubs, dirty needles, does pledge faithful an alignment recognizing players free and prestigious. These are all of my wishes now! Thus, this acknowledged transmission has so frustrated the MVP that he is readying for some act of terror.

Clyde. Did he send someone to Dawson?

Lord Bethea. Yes sir, with most certainty "Brother, not me," the salty errand boy shows me his rear and chirps, as you might say" For you, the time will be regretted that oppresses me with the response."

Clyde. It definitely could… give him a heads-up, whatever area his knowledge will give. Some saint rushed to New Jersey to translate the message before he arrives, so that immediate honors of worship will quickly come back to our anguished league. Held hostage to this wicked hand!

Lord Bethea. I will send supplication with him.

                                                  [Exit.]

*bombed: failed. Giants: baseball team in the Fairmount Park "A" League.

ACT FOUR: BOTTOM OF THE NINTH

SCENE 1

[A rundown playground, a wind swirled sandbox. Lightning. Appear the Three Shorties.]

First Shortie. Double twice the hairless dog does bark.

Second Shortie. One and double the warthog shrills.

Third Shortie. Boogeyman chirps "Let's do it," "Let's do it."

First Shortie.   Over and through the sandbox true.

Toss all venomous guts we'll do.

Bats that dwell in black draft cave

Through all eternity is night's slave

Simmering poison vanishing locks

Windstorm holds first within the box.

All.   No peace at work agitation twirl,

Now sand winds blow, now sandbox swirl.

Second Shortie.   Prime cut of rattler, with skin

Sling to the sandbox to blend in.

Snout of pig and hoof of camel,

Extract teeth of fish and mammal.

Fur of rat and maggots wiggle

Eye of hyena add too, the devilish giggle.

To the magical mix chaos strew,

From Hades storm, now winds brew.

All.   No peace at work, agitation twirl,

Now sand winds blow, now sandbox swirl.

Third Shortie.   Back of cockroach, fleas a many

Cigar of Groucho, glasses of Benny

All with the mauling artic bear Polar

Leaves of hemp which flourish in the solar.

Lips of gossip woman, so untrue,

Spleen of yak and rhino do-do.

Grayed by the wart cloud,

Ear of jerk and fools laugh aloud.

Naked bodies of just ripped snail,

Toilet grit from uncleaned jail.

Grease and grime now make it hearty,

Caked enough to serve at the party.

Add all thus to a lion mixed ox,

So it flows with the treacherous box.

All.   No peace at work, agitation twirl,

Now sand winds blow, now sandbox swirl.

Second Shortie.   Chill it with iced snot,

Now the potion's ready to be got.

[Enter Heatherkat, to the other Three Shorties.]

Heatherkat.   Baby I can dig it! I give you all props due,

Now folks with that, me will be credited too.

So, around this shape will I give bless,

Like angels winged and at the rest'

Delighting everything as all the best.

[Rapp song: "Drop it like it's hot" etc. Heatherkat vacates.]

Second Shortie.   From throbbing corns on my feet,

Comes this wretchedness we will meet.

Release the traps,

Bring forth whoever taps.

[Enter Willie.]

Willie. What's going on you dusty, dirty, and no daylight wags!* What you got!

All.   A portrait minus a face.

Willie. I know your incantations by that which you spout, what is the meaning to

whatever you dare, speak to me. Even if you let loose evils and allow them

battles unto the holy spirit halls; throughout the surfer' s pipe* confusing the

shoreline up and down. In spite of coconuts being shaken to fall, and grass

mowed short. In spite of laptops lodged atop their user's computer.* In spite of

spaces and places out there. Thou eyes affixed on the prize with stare. Of

natural rewards mixed all as one What evilness have you begun?

Speak to me, tell what is due.

First Shortie.   Word.

Second Shortie. Holla.*

Third Shortie.   Here it is.

First Shortie. Mention, if you want to hear it from our lips flow. Perhaps from the one

who floats our boat.

Willie. Summon the one, let me peep'em.

First Shortie. Throw in horse manure, for salad sweet

now jumble and tumble for re ady to eat, from the executioner's chambers

throw into the fire.

All.   Travel far or near,

your life's video you will see and hear.

[Lightning. Premonition Primero: baseball bat Chested.*]

Willie. Let me know something, thou mystical mystic---

First Shortie.   He's screened your brain. Listen without uttering a word.

Premonition Primero. Willie! Willie! Willie! Look out for Dawson, Watch out for the Commander of

South Beach. Bounce* me. Bastante!*

Willie. I'm not sure of what you are, however, thanks for the heads-up. You've tapped into my scare zone.

But give me one more taste.

First Shortie.   He's not gonna let you call the shots. Listen once more, it's more slammin'* than the first.

*wags: scandalous, rascal women. surfer's pipe: giant surfing waves ... Hawaii.
computer: head ... the ultimate computer heads. holla: (slang) call.

[Lightning. Premonition Segunda: needle in an Embryo.*]

Premonition Segunda. Willie! Willie! Willie!

Willie. If I had triple Bose,* I'd listen to thee.

Premonition Segunda. Be DNA rich and strong, smile to indignation

The forces of mankind, for no one conceived in female natural, shall hurt Willie.

[Coming down.]

Willie. Then let Dawson survive. What's my scare of it? However, I'll do triple somersaults making extra sure, and make a deadly promise.* He'll not survive; thus, I'll sing faded love

scare it rests, and slumbers in the wake of lightning.

[Premonition Tercero: A Baby wreathed,* with a rattlesnake about his feet.]
What the hey is this

That ascends the point or matter of a ruler, and is placed visual up on the baby's

crown, the circle of supreme pageantry.

Todas. Observe, yet utter not upon it.

Third Premonition. Be elephant robed, majestic and pay it no mind if anyone is

irritated, anyone vexes, or

where the haters may be.

Willie will not be conquered until Den Rattlers strike on FAMU's

High Hill to challenge and oppose him.

[Recoils.]

Willie. That ain't never gonna happen.

Who can charm the serpent, with the watch to scale the high from its base?

Sugary predictions! Bueno!*

Oppositions' hand, ascends not until rattlers of FAMU strike, and the noble-

sighted MVP covers his entire

lifeline. Compensate his air to minutes, hours and the human tradition.

However, my brain pulses to savor

just this thing. Chirp to me, if these sketches can clarify so many. Will Hartie's

matter come to the throne in this domain?

*baseball bat chested: chest with a bat sticking out... symbol of Dawson. Bounce:
(slang) dismiss. Bastante: sp. enough. slammin': powerful. Embryo: Dawson's birth.
Bose: stereo speakers. promise: insuring he'll kill Dawson.
Baby wreathed: symbol of Monty.

Todas. That's all for now, you yearn to know it all.

Willie. This will leave me full. Not telling me, thus an infinite misfortune will befall

you! Give up the info. Why

submerges the batting cage? Tell me what are these echoes?   [Bat boys.]

First Shortie.   Reveal!

Second Shortie.   Reveal!

Third Shortie.   Reveal!

Todas. Appear before his lens and break his heart.

Enter like images, so exit art!

[An appearance of nine All-Stars* the final with a reflector in his possession, Hartie's Spirit trailing.]

Willie. Each one takes on the replica of Hartie. Avaunt! Thy stars do burn my pupils. And their mustache, the other dark-adjoining goatee is presented like the primero. The third is like the one before. Dirty broads! What has possessed you to show me this? A number four! Commence, vision! Will the column expand through till Kingdom come? Here's more! An eighth! I won't bear to look. And still a ninth shows carrying a reflector telling me that more follow, and some I see the Columbia blue and red stallion head* toting. Terrible vision! I now know the deal, for the face cracked Hartie laughs at me, and summons thus by his. [premonition disappears.] How, is this to be?

---

*Bueno: sp. good. nine All-Stars: mocking stars at each position. Columbia ... heads: colors and insignia of the Mustangs.

First Shortie. Yeah boy, you betcha ain't nothing but a thang. Yet, you do be perched so shocked? Proceed, Siblings, party us down his spooks* thus reveal the better be our treats. I'll fancy the atmosphere to bring forth hearing whilst you execute the voodoo stomp.* So that this awesome ruler can say confident as heck, our responsibilities absorbed his greeting compensate.

[Video. The Shorties prance, and disappear, with Heatherkat.]

Willie. Which way did they go? Dismissed? Allow this perilous moment anchor yes damnation within the twelve months. Enter within, without here!

[Enter Clyde.]

Clyde. Your Majesty, what is your command?

Willie. Gazed you upon the scallywags?

Clyde. I did not your Grace.

Willie. They did not pass you?

Clyde. No way, Jose.

Willie. Tarnished is the atmosphere upon which they fly and bedeviled to everyone that credits them! I did harken the roaring of motors. Who was it at the visit?

Clyde. Twas several, my MVP, to give you say that Dawson has jetted to Miami.

Willie. Jetted to Miami! Yes sir my great star.

Willie. [corner of the mouth] Was then, you expected my awful acts. The skittish intention not to be surpassed. Perchance the plan be with it. As of this very second, the absolute premiers of my bosom is thus the premiers of my glove. 'Whilst presently, to anoint my ideas with deeds, so let it be envisioned and performed. The mansion of Dawson I'll astonish, grab up Bonsai,* face to the round barrel of the gun his spouse and his offspring, and all other unlucky spirits that come from within his lineage. Nor crowing like a peacock, these acts

I'll perform before this intention rests, oh the brain. However, do without the vision! Find me these hitmen! Hurry, show me their whereabouts.

SCENE 2

[Bonsai. Dawson's mansion. Enter Lady "D," her son and JoJo.]

spooks: spirits. voodoo stomp: grotesque dance. Bonsai: Dawson's mansion.

Lady "D." What had the brother done, thus making him fly the coop?

JoJo.   Just hold fast, mama.

Lady "D." There is no reason. His jetting is crazy. When the things we do don't, our
       scares can lead us to betrayal.

JoJo.   You cannot be sure if it was something intelligent or his dread.

Lady "D." Intellect! To abandon his soul mate, to denude his offspring of protection,
       his palace and belongings in a setting from hence he did jet? He does not
       cherish us, he craved the nature's feel. Yet, the hapless silkworm the tiniest of
       larva will spin to defend youth in her cocoon, against the woodpecker.
       Everything is the scared and nothing is the cherished, thus not much intellect,
       seeing the escape running counter to best judgement.

JoJo.   My closest kindred,* I hope you dig yourself, if only for your man. The brother
       is worthy of high praise, smart, makes good decisions and "daddy" knows best.
       It's a sign of the times. I'm afraid to rap too deeply. However, woe are the hours

when we are Benedict Arnold, thus we cannot be sure, when hearsay is rampant based on a fear even though we can't say what it is we're afraid of, however floats upon an untamed and turbulent tornado, every toss is about, and with thrust. I'm ready to roll from here now, however, it won't be too lengthy of a time before I return. The worst that could happen is that events come to an end, or perhaps begin to ascend to the status that they were previous. [To the youth] My most handsome cuz,* peace be with you.

Lady "D." He is baby daddied, and thus, he is baby daddyless.

JoJo.   I'll be more the "bellows bag"* If I linger anymore time. The shame would be mine and of your uneasiness. Therefore, I'm out with the quickness.

Lady "D." Sal, your daddy is deceased. At this moment do you have arrangements? How do you plan to survive?

Son.   As fish do, mom.

Lady "D." What, with goldfish and guppies?

Son.   By any means necessary, I think, and they do too.

Lady "D." Pityfull fish! You know not how to fear the mesh or hook! The trap nor the snare.

*kindred; cousin. cuz: cousin. bellows bag: OE belg, bag... fool Lat. follis, bellows.

Son.   For what reason, Mom? Valueless fish are not regarded. My dad is alive, in spite of everything that you say.

Lady "D." No, he's not alive. What will you do about a daddy?

Son. Not, what will you do about a spouse?

Lady "D." Yo! I can pick me up thirty at any club.

Son. Thus, you'll pick'em to betray them once more.

Lady "D." You talk with all your reasoning, still I believe you have reasoning enough for yourself.

Son.   Did my daddy mirror Benedict Arnold, mom?

Lady "D." You've hit the nail on the head.

Son.   Who was Benedict Arnold?

Lady "D." Well, someone who curses and deceives.

Son. And all are Benedict Arnold that do this?

Lady "D." Everybody that does this is a Benedict Arnold and has to be jailed.

Son. And should those that curse and deceive all be jailed?

Lady "D." Todo!

Son. They will be jailed by who?

Lady "D." Well, by the noble men.

Son.   Then the cursers and deceivers are "bellow bags," because there are more than a plenty of cursers and deceivers to whip-up on the noble men and jail them.

Lady "D." Presently, Jesus aid him, pitiful chimp! However, what are you gonna do about a daddy?

Son.   If he verily were deceased, you'd be crying now. Since you aren't, I believe that is a great indication that soon and very soon I'll have a new daddy.

Lady "D." pitiful chatterbox, oh how you speak'st

[Enter a Bearer.]

Bearer. To you good madame. I give blessings! You do not know me, nevertheless, in all of your glory, I am true.* I believe that you are about to come across some type of catastrophe. Suppose you just take the heed of wisdom from this dumb hombre. Make use of the get away with your babes from this palace. By scaring you, I surmise I am too harsh. Yet, anything more inferior would be a crying shame. Oh, it is very much near you, may the skies keep you! I must roll away immediately.

Lady "D." Away to where? I have not brought injury to anyone. Yet now, I do recall that in the mist of this worldly planet, where sometimes doing injustice ispraised, and doing virtuous is perceived as a lack of prudence. Perhaps then, oh well, should I just put up a female repellent and utter," I've caused no injury"?

[Enter Killers.]

First Killer. Your spouse, where is he?

Lady "D." I pray in no space of non-sanctuary being thus that you may discover him.

First Killer. He is Benedict Arnold.

Son.   That's bull you low life scoundrel!

First Killer. What, you seed!

Early plant of treason.   [Shooting him.]

Son. Mom, he has lullabied me. I pray today, you jet away!   [Expires.]

[Exit Lady "D.", wailing "Homicide!" Exit Killers, trailing her.]

SCENE 3

[Philadelphia. In front of the Royal's Mansion. Enter Monty and Dawson.]

Monty. Come on man, let's find a private obscurity where we can cry out the hurt in
   our chest.

Dawson. Instead, don't be quick to the trigger, be like nobles, stand with our befallen
heritage. * Every virgin sunrise a young wife screams, a youth without parents yells,
fresh heartaches thrust the celestials to their face, so it reverberates as if it could feel
alongside the big league, and roar out like sounds of torture.

*in... true: I know you to be honorable. heritage: born into baseball.

Monty. That which I believe to be, I will bemoan, what certain, accept. And things I
   can remedy thereby, I will encounter the minutes to acquaintance, * I'll do.
   What you have said, it could probably be, perhaps. This dictator the very sound
   of his call* irritates our ears, once to be perceived of as faithful. You've
   embraced him lovingly; he has not left his mark on you just yet. I am infant,
   however things owed of him you may have through me, the knowledge of
   sacrificing a faint defenseless calf to make concession with an enraged deity.

Dawson. I am not dangerous.

Monty. However, Willie is A fine and moral character may falter at a royal command.
However, begging your pardon. The things that be you, my brain will not remake.
Heavenly guardians shine on, still the shiniest came down. Yet, many items of error
would have the tag of true, still truth must sound thus.

Dawson. I cannot find any aspiration.

Monty. You know somehow, I'm having a little problem with that. Why in this crazy
   state would you leave your wife and bud, your most valuable possessions, your
   heart and soul, leaving without-securing? I beseech you, don't let my prying be
   your disgrace, my own are protected. You may be perfectly satisfied, no matter
   what I discern.

Dawson. Breathless, breathless forsaken land. Awesome oppression, is surly to blame, for the greatness has not the courage to inspect thee. Display you your faults, oppressions privilege is authentic. Get along well

player. I am not the scoundrel that you believe me to be. For the whole team is in the clutches of this villain also, the historic league itself.

Monty. Don't take it personal. I'm not rapping because of being definitely afraid of you. I believe that our league is fallen below the surface. It sobs, its wounds run, and every virgin sunrise a cut is annexed to her injuries. Besides, I believe help is on the way to assist me in getting my just due. Yes, right here in the city I have the support of millions of good souls. However, having all this, when should I pounce on and chop the bullies sky,* or take to a bat and wear him out. This unfortunate league of mine will have more problems than it has ever had, additional pain and many ways of it than before, under he that pans out.

Dawson. How stands he?

Monty. From within myself I know every in and out of corruption so implanted. Consequently, when they are revealed, ebony Willie will appear to be as right as rain, and the dreadful city endear him as a puppy, thus likened with my

*acquaintance: befriend. call: name. sky: head.

imprisoned injuries.

Dawson. Never in the brigades of hideous Hades will spawn a demon more hell bent in wickedness to ceiling

Willie. ·

Monty. I concede him intoxicatingly desirous, greedy, fake, lying, spontaneous, vicious, aromatic of all misdeeds that can be categorized. However, there is no end, nada within my desires of pleasure. Your spouses, your princesses, your servants, and your chaperones, could overflow the reservoir of my desire, and my want all world restrictions would take over anything that blocked my wish.

Be it with Willie than this type to rule.

Dawson. Infinite excessiveness by the natural is a crime, resulting in the unexpected vacating of the high seat and descent of many a Most Valuable. However, take not to scare, to go after that which belongs to you. You can transport your delights in knowing there's enough sky for everybody* and thus appear to moderate passion, the hour you might so bamboozle. To thus there are sufficient enough consenting broads.* There mustn't be a predatory in yourself to swallow up so many as destiny to excellence committed themselves discovering it much the tendency.

Monty. Somehow there is nurtured within my most sickly calm love this voracious greed, being if I were the MVP, I'd remove the owners from their stature status, acquire his treasures also, the remaining mansions and by my-acquisitions serving as the gravy making me to crave more, evoking me to thrust disputes unfairly towards brilliant and faithful, annihilating them for riches.

Dawson. This greed grabs depth, flowers with mucho destructive core likened to the passion of puppy love, and therein lies the thing that has killed our most high players. However, do not be afraid, the state has abundance to overflow yourwant, of your simple possessions. These can be withstood with additional honors tabulated.

Monty. However, this I have not, The MVP distinguishes like fairness, truth, restraint, firmness, harvest, effort, forgiveness, compassion, dedication, braveness, strength- I have no muster of them, however abundant with the separation of individual many fault, portraying it numerous paths. Not merely this, but also, if I owned but the energy, I would let flow the fine wine of harmony into Hades, uproot the galaxy of tranquility, put to confusion the whole of togetherness in the world.

*there's... everybody: enough room for your clandestine delights. broads: women

Dawson. My, My, My... Baseball, oh Baseball!

Monty. If that particular being be worthy to rule, say it. I stand with what I have said.

Dawson. Worthy to administrate! Nay, never to subsist. Oh nationality, sickened by the
    unauthorized seated menace brutally-baton, when should we look upon our
    good times once more. During the present time the true heir of the high seat's
    owner by his own absence postures sullied and does revile his own kind. Your
    majestic daddy was the noble ruler. The goddess that born you, bending more
    humbly than standing more proud, living to the most true yet, always prepared
    for the meeting with the Almighty. Good-bye! These calamities you've recurred
    upon yourself have ousted me from baseball. Oh my chest, the dream
    terminates aqui.*

Monty. Dawson, this illustrious love, Nino de moralidad* hath done with my spirit
    cleaned slated the ebony principles, making my thinking: friendly to your
    gracious right and dignity. Satanic Willie, through tons of these temptations
    does seek to draw me into his control also, moderate knowledge picks me out of
    over believing quickness. However, Christ overhead bargains among you and
    me. Right now, even I place myself to your guidance, and un-tongue my own
    self misrepresentations,* presently I reject solemnly the spoils and censures I
    lay over myself, for foreigners to my manner. Besides, I am anonymous to the
    ladies, being one hundred percent of my word, barely having covered that
    which was my possession at no point ever breaking with my faithfulness, would
    never give over to his fellow to the Satan, plus take pride nevertheless in
    fidelity than existence. The very premier of my artificial utterance, are these
    very words upon myself. To announce my real self, I am yours and this scanty*

city to direct to whatever place without question, in front of you now-comes, old man Hall with legions of star players chomping at the bit are pressing forward, now all as one, and the lottery of greatness be likened to our justification for argument! Why do you say not a word?

Dawson. Such wanted and unwanted charges at instance. It is difficult to adjust.

[Enter Doctor Johnson a Physician.]

Monty. Hmm, more at once. Is his Highness on his way, I ask you?

Physician. Yes sir, there's a bunch of tormented souls that are in need of his health magic, the bad warp of their minds alludes even the greatest of medicalknowledge. However, by his feel much calmness doth the divine sanctuary store within his palm, they immediately recover.

aqui: sp. here. Nino de moralidad: sp. moral child. misrepresentations: slander. scanty: poor.

Monty. Big ups,* Doc.

[Exits Physician.]

Dawson. Whatever ailment does he refer to?

Monty.   It's cited as the Alligator.*

A wonderous "trabajo de milagro"* within this kind Ruler. Having many times since I've been here in Gotham* City I've witnessed his performance. Thus, he incorporates the divine, he understands the better. However, unusual pop in folks totally puffed* and sored, dreadful to the sight, the very hopelessness of operation, he heals, placing a bling* bling necklace around their necks, placed about with divine words, in addition it's said, to the future next sovereign he bequeaths the prayer of recovery. That unusual beauty he possesses a divine present of foretelling predictions. Also, a plethora of prayers drape about his most highchair, that authors him "lleno de gracia."*

[Enter JoJo.]

Dawson. Yo! Look who's coming here?

Monty. My dog,* however, still I am not feeling him

Dawson. My cool cuz, come unto me. As-salaam- alaikam.*

Monty. Oh yeah, I recognize him right away. Good God y'all, vaya con Dios, in a minute wipe clean the clouds that forces us to be foreign to one another.

JoJo.   Bless you brother.

Dawson. Flys Philadelphia at the same height?

JoJo. Pitiful, wretched city! It is thus a foreigner to its own knowing. It cannot be nicknamed as our "Brotherly Love," only our deep six,* everything ain't everything, it used to be all that; where moans and grouch and ghoulish throaty, that scream through the atmosphere are trumped up, never trumped; where turbulent sadness appears to be a renaissance blockhead.* The grave man's bell, there's no script to track who's next, plus noble brother's existences' terminate "antes de la flora en el sombrero," expiring thus before they whither.

Dawson. That's the word, real, yet too surreal!

*ups: slang, thanks. alligator: refers to alligator skin, a rough tough cracking skin condition. trabajo de milagro: sp. miracle work. Gotham: New York City. puffed: swollen. bling: slang, diamond studded. lleno de gracia: sp. full of grace. dog: trusted one (slg.). As-salaam-alaikam: Muslim greeting, Dawson speaks many languages. deep six: grave. renaissance blockhead: rebirth of stupidity.

Monty. What is the latest lament?

JoJo. That is times olden, the latest ain't the greatest, because the latest becomes the
      fadest.* They pour every hour on the hour.

Dawson. And the well-being of my spouse?

JoJo. Quite the okay.

Dawson. Y mi ninos, todos?*

JoJo. Bien tambien.*

Dawson. The criminal hasn't wreaked havoc on their tranquility?

JoJo. Nadie, all were at smiles when I did last give gaze.

Dawson. Give me not the niggardliness of words. What is the deal spiel?

JoJo. When I journeyed to this spot to transmit the 411* which lies solidly within my
      chest, where flowest this hearsay of numerous players that were rising in an
      uproar, believe it, I saw it with my own eyes more exactly, with thus, I viewed
      the criminal's might a fist.* The time is right for plucking, your look to Philly
      should engender the hardballers, stir our softballers* to battle, to cast off their
      most deep-rooted fears.

Monty. Go to give them peace. We are following the sooner. Most worthy South Jersey
      has sent to our borrow high-grade "little Hall" and one hundred thousand
      hombres. A wiser and more gifted player there is nadie that Spiritualdom passes
      along.

JoJo. If I could play it, I'd say it. This peace would be the same. However, I have
      somechirps, that should be farted out into the atmosphere. Where the smelling
      shouldn't take hold to them.

Dawson. What are the issues? The overall acts? Or tis a costly distress,* outstanding by
      a one-sided chest?

JoJo. However, within fair portioned with grief, yo, listen up, the most of this stuff is
about you, yourself.

*the latest... fadest: there are so many crimes, one reported cannot be studied, fading
quickly into the next. Y... todos: sp. _And all my children. Bien tambien: well too. 411:
(slg.) information. a fist: all gripping. hardballers ... softballers: men's/women's
teams. Or... distress: personal sorrow.

Dawson. If you have something to say about me, come on with it. Hurry up, give it to
me!

JoJo. When you hear this, don't hate the player, hate the game.* I' am about to deliver
the roughest CNN* you've ever heard.

Dawson. O'okay, let me suppose at the thing.

JoJo. Your mansion has been startled, your spouse and offspring brutally butchered.
To give you an idea, were, ied* as are soldiers at war, of these waisted heroes, to
give addition to your demise.

Monty. My God! Yo, bro! Ne'er tug your hair to the roots. Release words of comfort.
This heavy burden that does not aloud itself, lip motions* the overloaded soul
and invitations it to spill.

Dawson. The kids also?

JoJo. Your lady, kids, hired help, all that could be located.

Dawson. And I the necessity to be from there! My life partner murdered tambien?

JoJo. As I have communicated.

Monty. Have strength. Let us go into pharmacy* to give mix to our awesome repay, to
sooth this lethal sorrow.

Dawson. The boy has no offspring. Todas de mi bonitas?* Did you mean not any left? Oh... Sugar-Honey-Iced-Tea!* Todo? Damn, every one of my furry bunnies plus their mom, at a single lightning strike?

Skip/Monty. Soldier that crap like a brother.

Dawson. I'll man up; However, I must endear it like a male. I only wish to bring to mind things as they were, those being the things that I cherish the most. Would the Gods have looked upon, and would not in their involvement partake?
Misdeeds of Dawson, they were all lost by me! Sin valor yo soy,* never for their genuine faults, no! However, por mi, disaster lay upon their bodies, may the peace be kept upon them now in heaven!

*don't... game: don't hate the messenger, hate the message. CNN: popular, reputable news channel of the day. ied: improvised explosive device, roadside bomb used in America-Iraq war. lip motions: whispers. pharmacy: store that sell soothing drug mixtures. Todas de mi bonitas: sp. all of my pretties. O'... Sugar-Honey-Iced-Tea! emphasis on Capitals. Sin valor yo soy: Worthless I am.

Skip/Monty. Allow this to become the sharpener of you long blade; allow sorrow to exchange to flame, debase not the hate of the heart, enliven it.

Dawson. Really, it would be possible for me to mimic the female with my own sight and boasts with my lips!

However, smooth clouds, slice the length of all interruptions. Cara a Cara* deliver thee that demon of Fairmount Park and me, to the range of my long blade's measure place him. In the event of his breakaway, may the God's have mercy on his soul also.

Skip/Monty. That note travels vociferously man. Vamanos,* to the MVP. Our might is right, our waste, imprisons time's haste. Willie is prime for the plucking, in addition, the beings overhead empower us to be their co-authors. Take pride in whatever accolade you might. The dark hours are not short when at no time can locate the dawn.

ACT FIVE: THE VICTORY

SCENE 1

[Fraternity House. Foyer in the domain. Enter a Specialist Doctor and an Attending Tenderhearted lady]

Physician. We have checked her for forty and eight hours, still I don't see anything real that was in your verbatim description. Ho, when was the last time she got to stepp'n?

Tenderhearted lady. Not since the MVP went to the contest.* I've witnessed her get out of her sack with her robe on, take a drink, get out a notebook, open it, jot down something, stare at it as if reading, zip lock it, and return to her bunk, without ever waking up from sleep.

Physician. A great crazy quirk of nature, to be able to cop some zzz's while participating in the benefits of awareness. Within this sleepy convulsion, in addition to her travels and her other real acts, ho, have you heard her do any talking?

Tenderhearted lady. Aye, aye capt'n, however, I can't give any quotes from her.

Physician. You can spill the beans to your boy, and it's important that you do.

Tenderhearted lady. Doc., I can't blab to you or nobody, no one was around to believe what I say.

*Cara a Cara: sp. face to face. Vamanos: sp. come, let's go. contest: to the game with the team.

[Enter Goldie, with a lantern.]

Quiet now, she steps this way! Observe to see her same pattern, plus, on my biography, deeply entranced.

Witness she. Be not seen.

Physician. Where did she get that lantern?

Tenderhearted lady. Well, it stays by her side. She consistently has a beam with her, it is her solemn order.

Physician. Mira,* her eyes are wide.

Tenderhearted lady. Seguro,* however, their understanding is nada.

Physician. What thing is this that she is exercising now? See she makes fast movements over and under with her hands.

Tenderhearted lady. O', tis her usual act, appearing to give the cleaning of her hands. I can attest to the fact that she goes on for fifteen solid minutes.

Goldie. Egad!* There's a blemish.

Physician. Listen! Her speech. I will take note of what she says, so that I can recall it more exactly.

Goldie. Oust, ye darn stain! Oust, I command! Uno, dos-perhaps now the moment to act upon it. Hades is turbid.

Bah humbug, my savior, bah humbug! A warrior, and scared? Why should we be afeared of the mysterious mystery, whilst nothing can bring our strength to accredit it? Still, would anyone have believed that the old timer would yield that tremendous amount of claret from within.

Physician. Did you record that?

Goldie. The Lord of Bonsai had a spouse What's her so-called whereabouts now?

What, will the blemishes ever be washed from these hands? Nevermore o' that, my savior, nevermore o' that. You've spoiled all with this beginning.

Physician. Exit, exit. You've witnessed that which you shouldn't have.

Tenderhearted lady. There she is uttering words that ought not be said, of this I am
positive. Only Celestial

Paradise has knowledge of what she has fathomed.

Mira: sp. Look, see. Seguro: sp. Sure. Egad!: astonishingly surprised.

Goldie. There, the feel of blood evermore. All the fragrances of Hawaii won't honey
coat this tiny palm. My, my, my!

Physician. What a murmur in place! The brain is lugubriously afflicted.*

Tenderhearted lady. I could not have such a brain in my mind but for the intellect of the
entire head.

Physician. Ding, dang, dong--*

Tenderhearted lady. Invocate to the heavens and hope that it is mister.

Physician. This infliction is beyond my expertise. Still, I've known others who have
strolled within their slumber who have passed away saintly in their futons.

Goldie. Scrub these palms, throw on your robe, appear not so ghostly. I repeat to you
over and over, Hartie is deep six, he will not rise from his tomb.

Physician. Thus so?

Goldie. A la cama, a la cama!* I hear banging at the entrance. Venga, venga, venga,
venga,* place your hand in mine. That which is finished cannot be unfinished.
A la cama, a la cama, a la cama.

Physician. Is she going back to retire now?

Tenderhearted lady. Immediately.

Physician. The filthy lowdown is being rustled everywhere. Out of nature acts will
beget out of nature headaches.

Sick mentalities unto their muted quilts shall exude their clandestine thoughts.
She necessitates more the holy help, than a doctors healing help. Lord, Lord
have mercy on everybody! See to her, separate her out of the ability to be hurt,
while still watching over her. Therefore, na night.* She has gotten me confused

in the head and bewildered in my witness. I ponder; however, I am afraid to talk.

Tenderhearted lady. Na night blessed Physician.

[Exit.]

scene 2

[The stadium near FAMU, Trumpets and flags, Enter Durant, Luke, Larry, Clyde, and Players.]

lugubriously afflicted: gloomy burdened. Ding, dang, dong: (slg.) well, well, well. a cama: sp. to bed. venga: sp. come. na night: (slg.) good night.

Durant. The League's might is close, in the charge is Monty, his cousin little Hall and the Hall of Famer

Dawson. The avenge fire is white hot within them, for their committed issues stand ready to the drug addicted and the fierce siren* electrify the living dead.

Larry. Not far from the Rattler Strike, that's where we will join them. It's the route that they are approaching.

Luke. Does anyone know if Tony comes with his brother?

Clyde. I know it to be exact, buddy, no he isn't. I have a list of all the aristocracy. There's little Hall's nephew, and a slew of young scrappies* that as we speak banter wildly for their graduation to men.

Durant. How goes the dictator?

Luke. Mighty FAMU he has stocked great power. Most bellow he's loco or crazy. Still others of disproportion despise him, do refer to it as heroic rage. However, this cat* is not able to zipper his mange within the pocket of control.

Larry. Presently, is he able to sense his clandestine homicides fogging around his hands. Every second rebellions criticize his trust violated. Those he gives mastery, shift only because mastered, nothing in amour. Currently, he doth notice his crown tilting slippery atop his head, like a giant sombrero on a half-headed burglar.

Durant. Name then the person who could fault his afflicted understandings to rewind and begin, during a time when everything embedded in him lends itself to condemnation thus for its own existence?

Luke. Advisably, we advance forward, to contribute conformity to places where it is honestly needed. Encounter us the cure of this ill prosperity,* in addition with him we rain down in our city's purification every drip of ourselves.

Clyde. Or the amount that is necessary, to roast the smooth peanut butter* while toppling the jelly.* For us, it is our steps toward FAMU.

[Exit stepping.]

SCENE 3

[FAMU. A club in the city. Enter Willie, Physician, and Renegades.]

siren: ready to the battle. young scrappies: (slg.) rookies. cat: guy ... (idiom). cure... prosperity: the cure (i.e. Monty and his bunch) that will heal the commonwealth. peanut butter: Skippy (Monty's nickname). jelly: Willie.

Willie. I'll have none of these excerpts, let them all bounce.* Till Rattlers fly towards FAMU I am not able to be infected with fright. How is the kid Skippy (Monty)? Did not woman give his birth natural? Those holy forces that fathom all of man's destiny have enunciated this to me. "Do not be scurred,* Willie, not any male that's delivered by female will ever reign supreme over me." Therefore, vamoose fake "a"* captains, and amongst the Philly connoisseurs. The brain I swing with in addition to the pulse I endure will not ever drag with uncertainty or quake me afraid.

[Enter an Attendant.]

Old Satan curse thee ebony, you coconut faced fool! Where did you get that duck gaze?

Attendant. There is a mighty one hundred thou---
Willie. Ducks, scoundrel?
Attendant. Players, mister.
Willie. Proceed to pierce your lips, plus under-scarlet thy fright, you knee-knocking kid. What players, sucka? Murder of thy mind! Those snowy jowls of yours are advisors to dread. What players, skim milk face?
Attendant. The Philly power so satisfy thee.
Willie. Get your mug the heck out of here.

[Exit Attendant.]

Lofton! ---I'm about to barf, when I gaze upon---Lofton, I shout! --- This surge will applaud me forever, or dethrone me right away. I have subsisted for a great period of time. My lifestyle has plunged into the charred, the fall tree, and all the things that should coincide with AARP,* as graying, dentures, all timers,* hordes of amigos. I realize this will never be, however, in their replacement, blasphemy, not boisterous but abysmal, voice cherished, respiration, which the lowly soul might gladly disown, plus challenge not. Lofton!

[Enter Lofton.]

Lofton. What is your want big dog?

Willie.   Any more news dispatched?

Lofton. Everything is made firm, which has been chronicled.

*bounce: walk on. scurred: (slg.) scared. "a": buttocks. AARP: organization for senior citizens. all timers: (slg.) Alzheimer's disease.

Willie. I will rumble till from my head my brain be smashed. Pass me my bullet proof vest.

Lofton. For the ready, however, not necessary for now.

Willie. I'll wear it anyway. Let fly extra equines, search through all the neighborhoods, shoot-up them that speak scared. Pass me my plated vest. What has become of the one within your treatment Doc.? Physician. Not really that ill my liege, as much as she is bothered by heavy-present whims that rob her from her sleep.

Willie. Free her of that. Are you not able to console a brain disorder, suck from the recollection bank an anchored misery, demolish away the scripted worries of the mind, and bless it with some fresh unaware remedy remove pollution from the full breast* of those hazardous things which fall heavy upon the heart?

Physician. With respect to that, the medical receiver must pastor to herself.

Willie. Hurl prescription to the wolves, I'm not hearing it. Here, fasten my plated vest to me, pass me my oozy.*

Lofton, ship out. Mr. MD, the captains have split from me. Here man, haste. If you have the power, Doc., calculate the atmosphere* of my kingdom, discover what plagues her, and bleach it to a sight and perfect prosperity, I will clap for thee till the very sound has reverberation, that would praise once more. Remove it at once, pray tell.* what aloe, ajax, or whatever Ex-lax* potion, would purge these Philly creeps from this place? Have you heard of them?

Physician. Yes sir, big dog, your always being to the ready allows us to know a little sum'n, sum'n.*

Willie. Come on with it I shan't fear the grim reaper or bombs, till Rattlers Den flies to

Tallahassee's highest hill.

Physician. [Aside] If I were free and clear from Talley Town's high hill... no amount of

money would ever lead me here.

[Exit]

SCENE 4

[Grounds near Rattlers Den. Tubas and costumes. Enter Monty, little Hall, and his Daughter, Dawson,

Durant, Luke, Larry, Clyde, JoJo and Players, strutt'n.]

full breast: bosom. oozy: high tech gun. calculate ... atmosphere: identify the sickness. Remove... tell: Willie orders Lofton to remove part of his ill fitted vest. Ex-lax: laxative. sum'n, sum'n: (slg.) something, something.

Monty. Family, I can feel that the times are all about us. The homes will be secure.

Durant.   We question it naught.

Little Hall. What den is this in front of us?

Durant.   The Rattlers Den.

Monty. Let every ballplayer diamondback his uniform and conceal amongst the

pattern.* Wherein we shall mirage the sum of our presence and allow detection

to be mistaken in the calculation of us.

Ball players. So let it be done.

Little Hall. Fact is, no one but that self- assured bully still resides in FAMU, and will

stand up to our assault upon it.

Monty. That is his only hope. For whatever benefit he thinks he has, nearly all

supporters and detractors have given him the rebellion.* In addition no one
pedestals him unless forced, nothing is the love, that's all missing from the bosom also.

Monty. Let us hold our blame until the battle is finished, and we've displayed
magnificent gamesmanship.

Little Hall. The hour draws upon us that will with appropriate judgement allow us to be
aware of that which we profess to possess, and what we have obligation to.
Thinking theorizes their doubtful dreams apply, however, particular element
strikes have to decide the direction with which to promote the battle.

SCENE 5

[FAMU. Within Lee Hall. Enter Willie, Lofton, and Renegades, with drums and costumes.]

Willie. Display out our trophies on the ivy fences. The shouts are thus "They roll." Our
fortress' power shall giggle an attack to despise. Put them to the down here till
drought and sickness swallow them whole. They've been re-cannoned with
people that were once ours, we could have encountered them boldly chest to
chest, and vanquished them in areas to their houses.

[A cry of women within.]

That sound, what is it?

*pattern: to form a pattern of diamondbacks. nearly... rebellion: both classes of people
higher and lower have deserted Willie*

Lofton. It is the wail of females, my leader.

Willie. I can barely recall the touches of horror. There was a time when my big five*
might have iced upon tasting a midnight cry, and my flesh would crawl at a
depressed tale sweaty and clammy like living was within.

For me, I have been nourished to the brim with misery. Disaster acquainted with my massacred thinking

must not now suddenly surprise me.

[Reenter Lofton.]

From whence came that shriek?

Lofton. Your Lady big dog, is expunged.

Willie. Death is her fate; nobody gets out alive. The spoken word would normally
command a space. The day After, and after, and after slithers upon the trivial
walk from twenty-four seven to twenty-four seven, to the final utterance of
video chronology, and all of our pasts have florescent clowns the path to dingy
curtains.* Exhaust, exhaust, short taper! This living is just a hoofing phantom,
an insufficient batter, that swaggers and worries his moment in the box and thus
is seen no more. It is a story transmitted by a fool chock full of light and power
reflecting zero.

[Enter news Bearer.]

You are here to extract from the mouth, the account and swiftly.

Bearer. Good heavens my chief, I have to reveal all that I have witnessed, however, I
am not certain how to bring it on.

Willie. Just, do it, man.

Bearer. While I was at my post upon the highest mound, I gazed in the direction of the
den, and behold I thinketh the rattlers began to take air.

Willie. False lexicon, property!*

Bearer. I will withstand your vengeance if it be a lie. Over the next horizon you shall
see them coming, I profess, a maneuvering proliferation.

Willie. If you give untrue accounts, over the nearest cliff shall you be tossed while still breathing till thirst dissolves you. If your words be righteous, it matters not,

big five: senses. curtains: death. False... property: untrue language...s1ave.

if the same is done for myself. I have mustarded the courage and started to question the gossip of the demon that falses like justice. "I will not panic, till Rattler's rattle and fly in the direction of FAMU." Load, load, and go! If what he affirms does come true, there is no running or dallying about. I'll start to take notice of the stars and hope the status of the universe were presently unfixed Flash the warning light! Quake, earth! Here, smash! At the minimum we'll perish with plated vest to our chest.

SCENE 6

[FAMU. In front of the campus. Bands and majesties. Enter Skip/Monty little Hall, Dawson, and their Legions, covered with snakeskin.]

Skip/Monty. Yo, we're plenty up on them, your scale slithers strip them from you, and reveal ourselves for who we be. Usted,* most valuable Unk,* will with my cuz, your left worthy seed, charge the opening combat. Capable Dawson and all of us will seize on everything that's left to fulfill, in keeping with our command.

Hall.   May success be with you. What will we encounter the dictator's strength this night, take us for losers, if we fail to rumble.

Dawson. Sound all of our drums with voice, provide them all life, those vociferous couriers of claret ant fatality.

[Exit.]

SCENE 7

[Another area of the grounds, Sirens. Enter Willie.]

Willie. They have knotted me to a post, being unable to flee, however, lion like, I will contend till the final bell. Where is he that was not conceived by female o' natural? Is this the person that I am supposed to be afraid of or not?

[Enter little Hall's daughter.]

Young Hall. Como se llama*

Willie. You would be dreaded to know it.

Young Hall. Forget that, I understand that you reference yourself with an appellation more ardent than any that is in Hades.

Usted: sp. you. Unk: (slg.) uncle. Como se llama: sp. What is your name?

Willie. Me llama is Willie. the "MVP."

Young Hall. Old Satan in the flesh cannot enunciate an ownership more abominating to
my sense of hearing.

Willie. Oh really, or more fearing.

Young Hall. You speak untruths, filthy fiend. With my A-K* I'll authenticate the
canard* that you utter.

[They begin blasting. Little Hall's daughter dies]

Willie. She was conceived by female naturally. However, guns I snicker at, arsenals
amuse me to despicableness, sported by people that are conceived of a woman.

[Exit.]

[Sirens. Enter Dawson.]

Dawson. That hubbub, it directs. Fiend, reveal thy kisser!* If you be so killed and with
no effort by me, my spouse and off spring's apparition will torment me
further. I will not battle with hired assassins, whose guns are paid to show
their power. It is you, Willie, or perhaps my gun, with a stilled barrel, I'll
holster once more unused. Here you should be, upon this loud noise, single of
awesome sound appear advertised. Please allow me to come upon him, Fate!
And I will panhandle no more.

[Exit Sirens.] [Enter Monty and Little Hall.]

Little Hall. Here, my All-Star, the campus is softly relinquished. The despot's
peeps all over do rumble, the talented players do courageously in the conflict,
this twenty-four seven is nearly yours for the ownership, there's not much else
to perform.

Monty. Thus, we have encountered with enemies who now rumble alongside us.

Little Hall. Step, man, upon the campus.   [Exit Sirens.]

SCENE 8

[Another part of the college park. Enter Willie.]

Willie. It is with question, that, why should I portray the Idi Amin,* and expire upon
    my own gun? Whereas I view exists, the slashes fixed mo better on them.

*A-K: lethal high-powered gun. canard: lie. kisser: face. Idi Aimn Dada: exiled
African tyrant presumed suicide or murdered.

[Enter Dawson]

Dawson. One eighty, crypto* cat, one eighty!

Willie. Above every other man, you I have dodged. However, back it up, and jump!
    This spirit o' me is overly electric with the claret of you anyway.

Dawson. I am without vocabulary. My say is my gun, you bleeding despot than idoms
    can distribute you out!

[They fight.]

Willie. You've mislaid work. As effortless as you might the furrowed* flame with your
    fancy gun imprint to break open my sacred temple. Lay down your mac- 10* on
    assailable domes.* I possess an enchanted existence, which cannot succumb to
    one conceived by female.

Dawson. Hopeless, is your enchantment, and allow the innocence that you still minister
    to inform you Dawson no doubt, from his mamma's belly was inconveniently
    hacked.

Willie. Damnable is that mouth that has informed me thus, because it has chickened*
the majority piece of hombre! And thus are these twisted sisters aka-shorties all
the more the liars that haggle alongside us in a twin manner, that maintain the
acts of covenant to our eyes, plus cleave it to our aspire. I refuse to have a
shoot-out with you.

Dawson. Then submit yourself, chicken, and survive and be the act and gape of the era.
We will display thee, as our exceptional freaks pictured on a poster and
captioned," Reward if you see this scoundrel."

Willie. I will not submit, to sniff the ground in front of the youthful Monty's foot, and
in addition be lured with the poor people's damnation. Though Great Rattlers do
slither atop FAMU's High Hill, and you countered, having not been conceived
from female, still I will attempt the final. Ahead of my vessel I cast my
belligerent escutcheon.* Proceed further, Dawson, and to him be cursed that
bellows "No mas!"*

[Exit, shooting. Sirens.]

[Withdrawal. Flourish. Enter, trumpets and flags, Monty, Little Hall, JoJo, and
Captains, and All-Stars.]

Monty. I hope that the buddies we've omitted do blow in* secure.

Little Hall. Some must be buried by war, and still, with this I view, so fantastical an
hour

*crypto: hidden secrets. Willie is a guy (cat) with secrets from hell. furrow: dug into
the earth (path). mac-10: automatic assault weapon. assailable domes: heads
vulnerable to attack. chickened: scared. escutcheon: shield. No mas: sp. no more. blow
in: arrive.*

as thus is inexpensively purchased.

Monty. Dawson is absent, and your honorable female seed.*

JoJo.   Your female seed, my liege, has compensated a warrior's obligation. She merely existed until she became a woman, still not quicker than her heroism authenticated in the unflinching position* where she battled. However, as the mirror of a woman, she passed on.

Little Hall. You mean she is defunct?

JoJo.   For shizzle,* and carried from the turf. Your reason of mourn should not be gauged by her value, because it is infinity.

Little Hall. Were her wounds in the frontal?*

JoJo. Yes, in the frontal.

Little Hall. Therefore, the Lord's warrior is she! Had I possessed the sum total of female seeds as I own follicles, I could not bless upon them all a more just end, and so her bell is rung.

Monty. She is valued more grieving, and I'll dollar that towards her.

Little Hall. Her current value is anon. The word is that she transitioned nicely, and anted up on the tally.* And thus, the peace of the Lord be with her! We're being approached by a fresher amenity.

[Renter Dawson, with Willie's dome.]

Dawson. Salutes, majestic Monarch! For you are thus so. Gaze here postures the false MVP's damned dome. The league is liberated. I envision you enveloped by the All-Stars of Zion,* that sing my greeting in and of their heads, whose vocals I want shouted alongside mine: Salute, MVP of Philadelphia!

Everyone.   Salute, MVP of Philadelphia!

Monty. I will not extend a vast portion of this hour before I calculate upon your many passions, and distribute that which is due you. My captains and players, from this point on be stars, the premier that ever Philly with stated homage has ever christened. What is further to accomplish will be cultivated freshly within time,

female seed: daughter. Unflinching position: standing firm when she fought Willie. For shizzle: (slg.) for sure. frontal: in front, father knows she died fighting not fleeing. anted... tally: paid her dues. All-Stars of Zion: Monty's little league team.

like summoning to house our banished comrades and amigos from distant shores that escaped the clutches of spying totalitarianism, generating forward vicious preachers of this deceased annihilator and his devilish head Lady, where, it is believed, by her lonesome and with wicked hands, did eradicate the one life of hers- that and what additional is required, this signals to us, by the glory of God we shall act in full rhythm, at correct hour and space. Therefore, appreciations to everyone at the same time and to every individual, to whom we do give invitation to view and witness our coronation at Delilah's.*

[Waving. Exit.]

Loud voice from the crowd.   "ees da sa sussaway"*

Delilah's: famed Philadelphia restaurant. ees da sa sussaway: let's get started. Signature greeting of Chief Halftown Traynor Ora Halftown from Seneca nation in NY State. Native American entertainer who hosted a children's show. Born on the Allegheny Indian Reservation, NY.

EPILOGUE

So thus, it was settled, through all the strife and pain The league though left smarting, was restored to fine reign Those good Gods of baseball, threw fast balls to counter curves To stand tall before them, took strong courage and deep nerves Now rise all ye faithful, of the old diamond game true Arise and play hearty, as if you all understood and you all knew This legend thus ends on a cool and powerful poetic glee With restoration of the rightful star, Skipper the Monty

ACKNOWLEDGEMENTS:

I would like to acknowledge the following individuals for their unique time and effort for helping to assist me in bringing Cambeth to fruition.

1. Ronisha Trower ………………………….. Editing
2. James J.T. Montgomery …………………. Photography/ Computer Analysis
3. Stephen Mathews ………………………… Script Consultant
4. Sterling Forth …………………………….. Illustrations
5. Angelise M. Rouse, Ph. D ……………….. Friend: Owner of Especially for
   Me Publishing Company

*A special thanks goes to my loving wife of 39 years for her inspiration and constant encouragement over time to get this book done. Thank you, Janice R. Montgomery.
Also, I would like to give a shoutout to the city and community of Camden, New Jersey, the school system and the wonderful students for whom I had the pleasure of serving as a teacher of English for 42 years.*

Muchas Gracias